Marcy R. Adelman, PhD
Editor

D0401658

Midlife Lesbian Relationships: Friends, Lovers, Children, and Parents

Midlife Lesbian Relationships: Friends, Lovers, Children, and Parents has been co-published simultaneously as *Journal of Gay & Lesbian Social Services,* Volume 11, Numbers 2/3 2000.

*Pre-publication
REVIEWS,
COMMENTARIES,
EVALUATIONS . . .*

More pre-publication
REVIEWS, COMMENTARIES, EVALUATIONS . . .

"**A** FINE COLLECTION OF ES-
SAYS. . . . [The women in
this book] share a marked distinction from the closeted and fearful
generation that preceded them and
the queer . . . generation that followed. These essays delineate the
accomplishments of these women
as well as the stresses and pressures they face. Of interest not
only to mental health professionals, but to all lesbians in their
middle years and any reader interested in lesbian life."

Lillian Faderman, author
To Believe in Women: What Lesbians
Have Done for America–A History

"**L** ONG OVERDUE. Considers
issues such as rejection by
parents, death of parents, ex-lovers as enduring friends, and balancing the needs of children, parents, and partners. . . . Shows
how far we have come from the
early days of gay liberation, but
also how resilient and adaptive
we must continue to be in rede-
fining and nurturing our relationships. *Midlife Lesbian Relationships* reveals the complexitites of
present-day lesbian lives."

Margaret Cruikshank
*Adjunct Professor of Women's
Studies, University of Maine*

More pre-publication
REVIEWS, COMMENTARIES, EVALUATIONS . . .

"**A** GROUNDBREAKING
COLLECTION OF ESSAYS. . . .
REJOICES AND INFORMS. I highly
recommend this book to both lesbians who will love finding themselves in its pages, and to the
health care providers and counselors who work with them."

Ellen Cole, PhD
Professor of Psychology,
Alaska-Pacific University

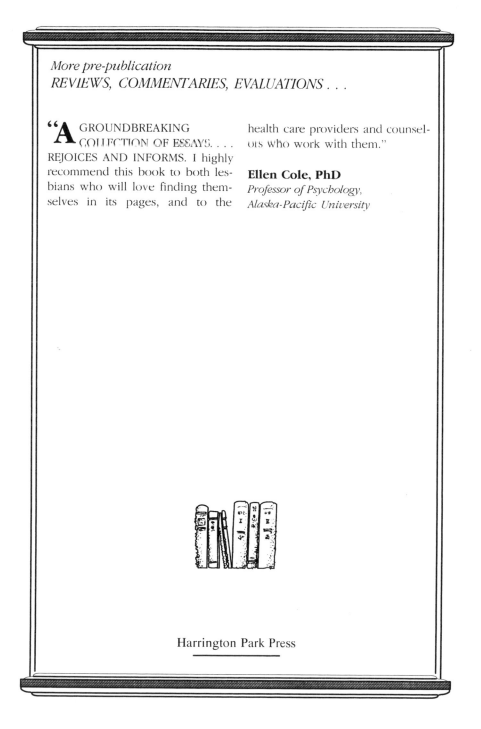

Harrington Park Press

Midlife Lesbian Relationships: Friends, Lovers, Children, and Parents

Midlife Lesbian Relationships: Friends, Lovers, Children, and Parents has been co-published simultaneously as *Journal of Gay & Lesbian Social Services,* Volume 11, Numbers 2/3 2000.

The *Journal of Gay & Lesbian Social Services* Monographic "Separates"

Below is a list of "separates," which in serials librarianship means a special issue simultaneously published as a special journal issue or double-issue *and* as a "separate" hardbound monograph. (This is a format which we also call a "DocuSerial.")

"Separates" are published because specialized libraries or professionals may wish to purchase a specific thematic issue by itself in a format which can be separately cataloged and shelved, as opposed to purchasing the journal on an on-going basis. Faculty members may also more easily consider a "separate" for classroom adoption.

"Separates" are carefully classified separately with the major book jobbers so that the journal tie-in can be noted on new book order slips to avoid duplicate purchasing.

You may wish to visit Haworth's website at . . .

http://www.haworthpressinc.com

. . . to search our online catalog for complete tables of contents of these separates and related publications.

You may also call 1-800-HAWORTH (outside US/Canada: 607-722-5857), or Fax 1-800-895-0582 (outside US/Canada: 607-771-0012), or e-mail at:

getinfo@haworthpressinc.com

Midlife Lesbian Relationships: Friends, Lovers, Children, and Parents, edited by Marcy R. Adelman, PhD (Vol. 11, No. 2/3, 2000). *"A CAREFUL AND SENSITIVE LOOK at the various relationships of [lesbians at midlife] inside and outside of the therapy office. A useful addition to a growing body of literature." (Ellyn Kaschak, PhD, Professor of Psychology, San José State University, California, and Editor of the feminist quarterly journal* Women & Therapy*)*

Social Services with Transgendered Youth, edited by Gerald P. Mallon, DSW (Vol. 10, No. 3/4, 1999). *"A well-articulated book that provides valuable information about a population that has been virtually ignored. . . ." (Carol T. Tully, PhD, Associate Professor, Tulane University, School of Social Work, New Orleans, Louisiana)*

Queer Families, Common Agendas: Gay People, Lesbians, and Family Values, edited by T. Richard Sullivan, PhD (Vol. 10, No. 1, 1999). *Examines the real life experience of those affected by current laws and policies regarding homosexual families.*

Lady Boys, Tom Boys, Rent Boys: Male and Female Homosexualities in Contemporary Thailand, edited by Peter A. Jackson, PhD, and Gerard Sullivan, PhD (Vol. 9, No. 2/3, 1999). *"Brings to life issues and problems of interpreting sexual and gender identities in contemporary Thailand." (Nerida M. Cook, PhD, Lecturer in Sociology, Department of Sociology and Social Work, University of Tasmania, Australia)*

Working with Gay Men and Lesbians in Private Psychotherapy Practice, edited by Christopher J. Alexander, PhD (Vol. 8, No. 4, 1998). *"Rich with information that will prove especially invaluable to therapists planning to or recently having begun to work with lesbian and gay clients in private practice." (Michael Shernoff, MSW, Private Practice, NYC; Adjunct Faculty, Hunter College Graduate School of Social Work)*

Violence and Social Injustice Against Lesbian, Gay and Bisexual People, edited by Lacey M. Sloan, PhD, and Nora S. Gustavsson, PhD (Vol. 8, No. 3, 1998). *"An important and timely book that exposes the multilevel nature of violence against gay, lesbian, bisexual, and transgender people." (Dorothy Van Soest, DSW, Associate Dean, School of Social Work, University of Texas at Austin)*

The HIV-Negative Gay Man: Developing Strategies for Survival and Emotional Well-Being, edited by Steven Ball, MSW, ACSW (Vol. 8, No. 1, 1998). *"Essential reading for anyone working with HIV-negative gay men." (Walt Odets, PhD, Author,* In the Shadow of the Epidemic: Being HIV-Negative in the Age of AIDS*; Clinical Psychologist, private practice, Berkeley, California)*

School Experiences of Gay and Lesbian Youth: The Invisible Minority, edited by Mary B. Harris, PhD (Vol. 7, No. 4, 1998). *"Our schools are well served when authors such as these have the courage to* *highlight problems that schools deny and to advocate for students whom schools make invisible."* (Gerald Unks, Professor, School of Education, University of North Carolina at Chapel Hill; Editor, The Gay Teen.) Provides schools with helpful suggestions for becoming places that welcome gay and lesbian students and, therefore, better serve the needs of all students.

Rural Gays and Lesbians: Building on the Strengths of Communities, edited by James Donald Smith, ACSW, LCSW, and Ronald J. Mancoske, BSCW, DSW (Vol. 7, No. 3, 1998). *"This informative and well-written book fills a major gap in the literature and should be widely read."* (James Midgley, PhD, Harry and Riva Specht Professor of Public Social Services and Dean, School of Social Welfare, University of California at Berkeley)

Gay Widowers: Life After the Death of a Partner, edited by Michael Shernoff, MSW, ACSW (Vol. 7, No. 2, 1997). *"This inspiring book is not only for those who have experienced the tragedy of losing a partner-it's for every gay man who loves another."* (Michelangelo Signorile, author, Life Outside)

Gay and Lesbian Professionals in the Closet: Who's In, Who's Out, and Why, edited by Teresa DeCrescenzo, MSW, LCSW (Vol. 6, No. 4, 1997). *"A gripping example of the way the closet cripples us and those we try to serve."* (Virginia Uribe, PhD, Founder, Project 10 Outreach to Gay and Lesbian Youth, Los Angeles Unified School District)

Two Spirit People: American Indian Lesbian Women and Gay Men, edited by Lester B. Brown, PhD (Vol. 6, No. 2, 1997). *"A must read for educators, social workers, and other providers of social and mental health services."* (Wynne DuBray, Professor, Division of Social Work, California State University)

Social Services for Senior Gay Men and Lesbians, edited by Jean K. Quam, PhD, MSW (Vol. 6, No. 1, 1997). *"Provides a valuable overview of social service issues and practice with elder gay men and lesbians."* (Outword)

Men of Color: A Context for Service to Homosexually Active Men, edited by John F. Longres, PhD (Vol. 5, No. 2/3, 1996). *"An excellent book for the 'helping professions.' "* (Feminist Bookstore News)

Health Care for Lesbians and Gay Men: Confronting Homophobia and Heterosexism, edited by K. Jean Peterson, DSW (Vol. 5, No. 1, 1996). *"Essential reading for those concerned with the quality of health care services."* (Etcetera)

Sexual Identity on the Job: Issues and Services, edited by Alan L. Ellis, PhD, and Ellen D. B. Riggle, PhD (Vol. 4, No. 4, 1996). *"Reveals a critical need for additional research to address the many questions left unanswered or answered unsatisfactorily by existing research."* (Sex Roles: A Journal of Research) *"A key resource for addressing sexual identity concerns and issues in your workplace."* (Outlines)

Human Services for Gay People: Clinical and Community Practice, edited by Michael Shernoff, MSW, ACSW (Vol. 4, No. 2, 1996). *"This very practical book on clinical and community practice issues belongs on the shelf of every social worker, counselor, or therapist working with lesbians and gay men."* (Gary A. Lloyd, PhD, ACSW, BCD, Professor and Coordinator, Institute for Research and Training in HIV/AIDS Counseling, School of Social Work, Tulane University)

Violence in Gay and Lesbian Domestic Partnerships, edited by Claire M. Renzetti, PhD, and Charles Harvey Miley, PhD (Vol. 4, No. 1, 1996). *"A comprehensive guidebook for service providers and community and church leaders."* (Small Press Magazine)

Gays and Lesbians in Asia and the Pacific: Social and Human Services, edited by Gerard Sullivan, PhD, and Laurence Wai-Teng Leong, PhD (Vol. 3, No. 3, 1995). *"Insights in this book can provide an understanding of these cultures and provide an opportunity to better understand your own."* (The Lavendar Lamp)

Lesbians of Color: Social and Human Services, edited by Hilda Hidalgo, PhD, ACSW (Vol. 3, No. 2, 1995). *"An illuminating and helpful guide for readers who wish to increase their understanding of and sensitivity toward lesbians of color and the challenges they face."* (Black Caucus of the ALA Newsletter)

Lesbian Social Services: Research Issues, edited by Carol T. Tully, PhD, MSW (Vol. 3, No. 1, 1995). *"Dr. Tully challenges us to reexamine theoretical conclusions that relate to lesbians. . . A must read."* (The Lavendar Lamp)

HIV Disease: Lesbians, Gays and the Social Services, edited by Gary A. Lloyd, PhD, ACSW, and Mary Ann Kuszelewicz, MSW, ACSW (Vol. 2, No. 3/4, 1995). *"A wonderful guide to working with people with AIDS. A terrific meld of political theory and hands-on advice, it is essential, inspiring reading for anyone fighting the pandemic or assisting those living with it." (Small Press)*

Addiction and Recovery in Gay and Lesbian Persons, edited by Robert J. Kus, PhD, RN (Vol. 2, No. 1, 1995). *"Readers are well-guided through the multifaceted, sometimes confusing, and frequently challenging world of the gay or lesbian drug user." (Drug and Alcohol Review)*

Helping Gay and Lesbian Youth: New Policies, New Programs, New Practice, edited by Teresa DeCrescenzo, MSW, LCSW (Vol. 1, No. 3/4, 1994). *"Insightful and up-to-date, this handbook covers several topics relating to gay and lesbian adolescents . . . It is must reading for social workers, educators, guidance counselors, and policymakers." (Journal of Social Work Education)*

Social Services for Gay and Lesbian Couples, edited by Lawrence A. Kurdek, PhD (Vol. 1, No. 2, 1994). *"Many of the unique issues confronted by gay and lesbian couples are addressed here." (Ambush Magazine)*

Midlife Lesbian Relationships: Friends, Lovers, Children, and Parents

Marcy R. Adelman, PhD
Editor

Midlife Lesbian Relationships: Friends, Lovers, Children, and Parents has been co-published simultaneously as *Journal of Gay & Lesbian Social Services,* Volume 11, Numbers 2/3 2000.

Harrington Park Press
An Imprint of
The Haworth Press, Inc.
New York • London • Oxford

Published by

Harrington Park Press, 10 Alice Street, Binghamton, NY 13904-1580

Harrington Park Press is an imprint of The Haworth Press, Inc., 10 Alice Street, Binghamton, NY 13904-1580 USA.

Midlife Lesbian Relationships: Friends, Lovers, Children, and Parents has been co-published simultaneously as *Journal of Gay & Lesbian Social Services* ™, Volume 11, Numbers 2/3 2000.

The Haworth Press, Inc., 10 Alice Street, Binghamton, NY 13904-1580 USA

Library of Congress Cataloging-in-Publication Data

Midlife lesbian relationships: friends, lovers, children and parents/Marcy R. Adelman, editor.
    p. cm.
    "Has been co-published simultaneously as Journal of gay & lesbian social services, volume 11, numbers 2/3 2000."
    Includes bibliographical references and index.
    ISBN 1-56023-141-6 (alk. paper)–ISBN 1-56023-142-4 (alk. paper)
    1. Middle aged lesbians–United States–Family relationships. 2. Lesbian couples–United States. 3. Lesbian mothers–United States. 4. Children of gay parents–United States. I. Adelman, Marcy. II. Journal of gay & lesbian social services.
HQ75.6.U5 M53 2000
305.244–dc21
                                                          00-031966

INDEXING & ABSTRACTING

Contributions to this publication are selectively indexed or abstracted in print, electronic, online, or CD-ROM version(s) of the reference tools and information services listed below. This list is current as of the copyright date of this publication. See the end of this section for additional notes.

- *AIDS Newsletter c/o CAB International/CAB ACCESS www.cabi.org/*
- *BUBL Information Service, an Internet-based Information Service for the UK higher education community <URL: http://bubl.ac.uk/>*
- *Cambridge Scientific Abstracts*
- *caredata CD: the social and community care database*
- *CNPIEC Reference Guide: Chinese National Directory of Foreign Periodicals*
- *Contemporary Women's Issues*
- *Criminal Justice Abstracts*
- *ERIC Clearinghouse on Urban Education (ERIC/CUE)*
- *Family Studies Database (online and CD/ROM)*
- *Family Violence & Sexual Assault Bulletin*
- *FINDEX, a free Internet Directory of over 150,000 publications from around the world www.publist.com*
- *Gay & Lesbian Abstracts*
- *GenderWatch*
- *HOMODOK/"Relevant" Bibliographic Database*
- *IBZ International Bibliography of Periodical Literature*
- *Index to Periodical Articles Related to Law*
- *Mental Health Abstracts (online through DIALOG)*
- *Referativnyi Zhurnal (Abstracts Journal of the All-Russian Institute of Scientific and Technical Information)*
- *Social Services Abstracts www.csa.com*
- *Social Work Abstracts*
- *Sociological Abstracts (SA) www.csa.com*

(continued)

- *Studies on Women Abstracts*
- *Violence and Abuse Abstracts: A Review of Current Literature on Interpersonal Violence (VAA)*

Special Bibliographic Notes related to special journal issues (separates) and indexing/abstracting:

- indexing/abstracting services in this list will also cover material in any "separate" that is co-published simultaneously with Haworth's special thematic journal issue or DocuSerial. Indexing/abstracting usually covers material at the article/chapter level.
- monographic co-editions are intended for either non-subscribers or libraries which intend to purchase a second copy for their circulating collections.
- monographic co-editions are reported to all jobbers/wholesalers/approval plans. The source journal is listed as the "series" to assist the prevention of duplicate purchasing in the same manner utilized for books-in-series.
- to facilitate user/access services all indexing/abstracting services are encouraged to utilize the co-indexing entry note indicated at the bottom of the first page of each article/chapter/contribution.
- this is intended to assist a library user of any reference tool (whether print, electronic, online, or CD-ROM) to locate the monographic version if the library has purchased this version but not a subscription to the source journal.
- individual articles/chapters in any Haworth publication are also available through the Haworth Document Delivery Service (HDDS).

Midlife Lesbian Relationships: Friends, Lovers, Children, and Parents

CONTENTS

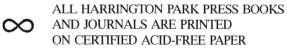

ABOUT THE EDITOR

Marcy Adelman, PhD, is a writer, researcher in lesbian and gay aging and a psychologist in private practice in San Francisco, California. She is editor of *Long Time Passing: Lives of Older Lesbians,* an anthology that presents the stories of old lesbians told in their own voices. She is a national leader of workshops on the psychotherapy of lesbian couples. Currently she is co-chair of Rainbow Adult Community Housing, (RACH), a non-profit organization committed to creating senior housing in the San Francisco Bay Area for the gay/lesbian/bisexual/transgender community.

Preface

This collection of essays has been compiled to expand our understanding of lesbians at midlife by exploring the complexities of relationships and bonds that sustain and nurture our lives. Since so many aspects of a woman's sense of self are embedded in her relationships, what better way to understand the issues facing lesbians at midlife than to explore our relationships to significant others. The articles in this volume spotlight relationships with friends, lovers, parents, and children and experiences with dating, recovery, and loss.

For most lesbian and heterosexual women, midlife is a positive, spirited time. Confident and established both in ourselves and in our communities, most women at midlife have constructed comfortable identities and lives. But midlife is also a time of change and growth uniquely informed by self-perceptions accumulated over half a lifetime of experiences and energized by the awareness of the finiteness of our lives.

Consolidation and expansion of self is the internal process of midlife development, and the external process is the reshaping of our lives to reflect and affirm a new midlife sense of ourselves. Thus, a common narrative among women at midlife which reflects this process is the acquisition of greater self-awareness and increased self-acceptance. Midlife tales typically involve transition and change, when a woman comes to terms with who she is through self-acceptance or through retrieving a self previously limited by family loyalties and/or cultural prescriptions of how she should live and age.

Change and personal growth can occur at this time of development in response to arriving where we intended to be and/or to losses and disappointments. Either impetus typically ushers in a period of reflec-

[Haworth co-indexing entry note]: "Preface." Adelman, Marcy R. Co-published simultaneously in *Journal of Gay & Lesbian Social Services* (Harrington Park Press, an imprint of The Haworth Press, Inc.) Vol. 11, No. 2/3, 2000, pp. xvii-xxi; and: *Midlife Lesbian Relationships: Friends, Lovers, Children, and Parents* (ed: Marcy R. Adelman) Harrington Park Press, an imprint of The Haworth Press, Inc., 2000, pp. xiii-xvii. Single or multiple copies of this article are available for a fee from The Haworth Document Delivery Service [1-800-342-9678, 9:00 a.m. - 5:00 p.m. (EST). E-mail address: getinfo@haworthpressinc.com].

tion and a revision of the life narrative. An important part of the midlife review is an acknowledgement of regrets, disappointments, and limitations, as well as gains, successes, and strengths. After a reappraisal of strengths and shortcomings, achievements and limitations, a woman may modify her life course only slightly or feel compelled to more dramatic action to match internal changes. This period of transition can be anything from a quiet contemplation and conscious and/or unconscious self-examination, to a topsy-turvy time of action and reaction fueled by an urgent awareness of our mortality. Patterns of this reconfiguration are wonderfully and endlessly diverse for both lesbians and heterosexuals. Valory Mitchell's article, "The Bloom Is on the Rose: The Impact of Midlife on the Lesbian Couple," describes how responses to the vicissitudes of midlife can alter and expand a lesbian's sense of self and her primary relationship. Jeanette Gurevitch's paper, "Filial Bereavement: Midlife Lesbian Daughters and Intersubjective Thoughts," discusses the impact of filial loss on the midlife development of lesbian daughters. Both articles have a clinical focus and illustrate issues with vignettes and quotes from clinical material.

To understand the unique midlife lesbian issues and adaptations discussed in this volume, it is important to understand some essential differences between lesbians and heterosexual women. Lesbian couples are of the same biological sex and therefore share the same gender socialization. Also, lesbian development is influenced by the degree of hostility towards lesbians in our culture and an individual's psychosocial skills and social resources available to deal with homophobia. It is here that the differences in midlife issues between lesbian and heterosexual women begin to emerge.

Much research has been done on the reversal of gender roles in heterosexuals at midlife. Heterosexual women are thought to expand their sense of self by reclaiming their assertiveness and autonomy, while heterosexual men are thought to do so by reclaiming the more relational parts of themselves. Lesbians at midlife who have lived their adult years in partnership with other women do not have a history of being constrained by traditional gender roles and hierarchies. This expansion of self at midlife by the reversal of gender roles does not occur with any great significance for lesbians. Lesbians between the ages of 40 and 60 years of age, as part of the baby boom generation, were able to take advantage of increased opportunities for women in work and education. This generation of women could develop both a vocational and lesbian identity and a life insulated from male hierarchies and separate from heterosexual domesticity.

Although liberated from the constraints of gender roles, lesbians continually confront the contingencies of stigma. Negative attitudes in our culture–for example, the stereotype that lesbians are psychologically and/or morally deficient–must be dealt with both internally and externally. Midlife lesbian expansion of self does not occur so much around the expansion of gender roles; rather, it occurs in response to those parts of the self that may have been abandoned, denied, muted, or enhanced as a response to internal and external homophobia. If a lesbian has spent her adult life believing parenting is the exclusive prerogative of heterosexuals, she may reevaluate this limitation and decide to parent or co-parent. If she has led a party life, often to deny the pain of marginality and oppression, she may retrieve a more sober and relational part of herself. Christa Donaldson's paper, "Midlife Lesbian Parenting," explores the issues of lesbian couples who have chosen to parent at midlife. She discusses themes that emerge from interviews she conducted in two separate studies 10 years apart. Finnegan and McNally's article, "Making Up for Lost Time: Chemically Dependent Lesbians in Later Midlife," is a description of the difficulties and issues encountered by lesbians at midlife who are just starting recovery and by lesbians who after many years of sobriety are experiencing a midlife transition.

Lesbians at midlife also have unique issues in the management of family relationships when they are called on to be care-givers to their elder parents. Issues concerning how the family of origin accepts a daughter's lesbianism and partner (if she has one) and the family history around these issues also will have profound impacts on these relationships. Raphael and Meyer, in "Family Support Patterns for Midlife Lesbians: Recollections of a Lesbian Couple 1971-1997," share their impressions and insights acquired over the course of their 26-year relationship.

Lesbians must juggle the painfully acute awareness of how discrimination impacts and limits our lives and our need to function in everyday life. Management of everyday life in a hostile and stigmatized environment requires disregarding this awareness and any accompanying feelings of anger, fear, and/or sadness and the compromises we feel compelled to make. These compromises include the "everyday" compromises, such as when and where to hold hands in public, as well as the bigger compromises, with ourselves and in our relationships, such as whether we should have children, how we are recognized by our family of origin, how we prioritize or don't prioritize our relationships, or what kind of careers we feel we can have. The midlife transition allows us to lift the veil from disregarded constraints and compromised responses to stigma and to examine anew the loss of heterosexual privilege and both the costs and benefits of the choices we have made. We are then able to take the opportunity to reshape our lives and our relationships to reflect and affirm a newly fashioned and more expansive midlife self.

A woman's assumptions and expectations about herself and others are shaped by sociohistorical circumstances as well as development. How lesbians construct identity, make adaptations, and form families differs from generation to generation. Generations raised in different sociohistorical circumstances are most likely to age differently because they will be presented with different opportunities and problems. A creative response to stigma in this generation of midlife lesbians, for whom family support was either absent or in some way diminished, is the importance of non-biological bonds. Friends and ex-lovers often have the emotional and role significance of family.

In previous generations, "lesbian" was primarily a sexual identity with an outlaw sensibility. An adaptive strategy in earlier times was to be nondisclosing and relatively uninvolved and unidentified with other lesbians. But being closeted–which was adaptive for one generation–became maladaptive for the next, when the meaning of being a lesbian was reconstructed in a broader, more encompassing identity. The baby boom generation of lesbians, who reached adulthood in the turbulent social and political changes of the 1960s and 70s, no longer saw themselves exclusively as sexual outlaws, but also as an oppressed minority. This identity shift allowed us to create positive communities based on woman-identified, feminist principles. It took most of our lives. We were well into adulthood before a positive view of lesbianism began to emerge in the mainstream culture. In this cultural context (i.e., a shift from repudiation to tolerance), we constructed our identities, formed our communities, and shaped our relationships with friends and significant others. Jacqueline Weinstock's article, "Lesbian Friendships at Midlife: Patterns and Possibilities for the 21st Century," provides an historic overview and asks whether these special relationships will continue to be an important part of lesbian extended family or whether they are, as an artifact of the historical context, unique to our generation.

Rose and Zand report on a comparative study of lesbian dating and courtship scripts across three age groups–young adult, adult and mid-life lesbians (ages 22-63). They identify major patterns of lesbian dating and courtship across the life cycle and report age-related differences in lesbian relationship formation.

Lesbian lives and narratives are rich with diversity. Lesbians live in different communities and have different priorities as to work, family and spirituality. We are diverse in our sexual and relational needs and how we express and experience those needs. We are single, or in long- or short-term relationships; we are parents, co-parents, and non-parents. We may be in various degrees of being out and/or closeted at work, to our families, and within our communities. We are of every racial and ethnic group and come from any class background. Such a heterogeneous group inevitably will have within it different experiences of aging and midlife. This volume is not meant to be comprehensive but is offered as just one small piece of the lesbian mosaic. There is much to know and celebrate about ourselves at midlife.

The generation of lesbians now at midlife is the largest generation of "out" lesbians to reach midlife. Because of sheer size and number, this generation most likely will use social services to a greater degree than at any other time in history to aid themselves, their friends, their parents, and/or their children. Social service providers need to be informed about the issues specific to midlife lesbians and not project mainstream models onto lesbians at midlife. It is important that providers understand the intricate network of lesbian relationships, recognize alternative models of relating and growing, and preserve the freedom to choose patterns of midlife development that best reflect personal desires and best fit within particular life choices and structures.

Marcy R. Adelman, PhD
Clinical Psychologist in Private Practice
San Francisco, CA

I am grateful for the warm support and constant encouragement of my friends and colleagues. First, I want to thank Jan Faulkner for our countless discussions about women and aging. A special thank you to Gina Clewley, friend and colleague extraordinaire, for her unflagging support. I would like to thank Ray Berger, my senior editor, for inviting me to do this book and for his helpful guidance. My thanks and appreciation to Elizabeth Robinson for her enthusiasm and copy-editing expertise. To Carla Golden, Janet Linder, Monique Barrault, and Marcy Gaugh, thank you all for your generosity and thoughtfulness. To the two Marcs in my life, Marc Adelman and Mark Gurevitch, thank you for your patience and support. My profound thanks to Emmanuelle Meynot whose heart and courage are always an inspiration to me. And my love and gratitude to Jeanette for her persistence and grace under pressure.

Marcy R. Adelman

Lesbian Friendships at Midlife: Patterns and Possibilities for the 21st Century

Jacqueline S. Weinstock

SUMMARY. This article examines current patterns and future possibilities for lesbians' friendships at midlife. Drawing upon the particular historical and developmental experiences of white, middle-class lesbians at midlife today, three patterns of "friends as family" are identified and explored: (a) friends as substitute family members, (b) friends as a challenge to the core family structure, and (c) friends as in-laws. While each friendship pattern reflects a valuation of friendships among midlife lesbians, each also holds unique implications for the organization and prioritization of midlife lesbians' other relationships and life choices. The existence of these diverse patterns of friendship has important implications for lesbians themselves, as well as for researchers, theoreticians, and social service practitioners working with midlife lesbians. *[Article copies available for a fee from The Haworth Document Delivery Service: 1-800-342-9678. E-mail address: <getinfo@haworthpressinc.com> Website: <http://www.haworthpressinc.com>]*

Jacqueline S. Weinstock, PhD, is Assistant Professor in the Human Development and Family Studies Program at the University of Vermont. The author would like to thank her friends, colleagues, and students who have shared in many wide-ranging and thought-provoking conversations about lesbians, midlife, friendships, lover relationships, parenting, and the development of nurturing communities. She would especially like to thank the following people for their contributions to the ideas reflected in this article: Marcy Adelman, Eileen Blackwood, Lynne Bond, Michelle Clossick, Diane Felicio, Dorothy Forsyth, Golda Ginsburg, Lynn Goyette, Kristi Hannan, Betsy Hinden, Josie Juhasz, Sallie McCorkle, and Esther Rothblum.

The author may be reached by post at the University of Vermont, C-150 Living & Learning Center, Burlington, VT 05405, or by e-mail at: jsweinst@zoo.uvm.edu.

[Haworth co-indexing entry note]: "Lesbian Friendships at Midlife: Patterns and Possibilities for the 21st Centtury." Weinstock, Jacqueline S. Co-published simultaneously in *Journal of Gay & Lesbian Social Services* (Harrington Park Press, an imprint of The Haworth Press, Inc.) Vol. 11, No. 2/3, 2000, pp. 1-32; and: *Midlife Lesbian Relationships: Friends, Lovers, Children, and Parents* (ed: Marcy R. Adelman) Harrington Park Press, an imprint of The Haworth Press, Inc., 2000, pp. 1-32. Single or multiple copies of this article are available for a fee from The Haworth Document Delivery Service [1-800-342-9678, 9:00 a.m. - 5:00 p.m. (EST). E-mail address: getinfo@haworthpressinc.com].

KEYWORDS. Lesbian, midlife, friendship, friends as family, substitute family, family of choice, family of origin, heterosexism, parenting, ageism, LBGTs

In the year 2000, those born between 1935 and 1961 will be between the ages of 40 and 65, ages that typically represent middle adulthood. Lesbians of these birth cohorts in the United States have witnessed tremendous changes in the images of and possibilities for living as lesbians. They spent their younger years in a pre-feminist and pre-gay liberation era, moved through young adulthood during the rise of the current feminist and gay liberation movements, and subsequently entered into midlife in the wake of the changes brought about by these movements. These combined historical and developmental contexts shaped midlife lesbians' conceptions and experiences of friendships. My aim for this article is to turn the spotlight on conceptions and experiences of friendship among some white, middle-class, midlife lesbians in the United States today. In particular, I present and examine three diverse patterns of "friends as family": (a) friends as substitute family members, (b) friends as a challenge to the core family structure, and (c) friends as in-laws.

Much of the available literature on lesbians in general and lesbians' friendships in particular has concentrated on the period of young adulthood. When friendships have been examined, the focus has been directed to the impact of friendships on lesbians' lover relationships. Little attention has been paid to examining the realities and possibilities of lesbians' friendships at midlife. Yet this phase of life may bring with it particular challenges to and perspectives on friends, family, and friends as family. Directing the spotlight onto lesbians' friendships at midlife may contribute to the construction of new frameworks for thinking about and working with lesbians, their friends, and their families, which may help better recognize and honor the many varied, overlapping, and often central roles that both friends and family may play in midlife lesbians' lives.

In constructing the three conceptions of "friends as family" outlined in this article, I have drawn upon a combination of resources, including theoretical analyses, empirical research, published personal reflections, and a small sample of interviews with self-identified lesbians in or nearing midlife, conducted as part of an ongoing study of the friendships of lesbians, gay men, bisexual women and men, and transgender persons (LGBTs). All of these sources draw upon and most accurately reflect the experiences of young adult, white, middle-class lesbians in the United States, who are publicly associated, at least to some extent, with LGBT cultural or political events and/or feminist movements. My own particular circumstances also reflect these experiences.

The patterns of friendship presented in this article, and their presence in midlife lesbians' lives today, clearly reflect a select population and a particular intersection of historical time and cohort. The stories of friendship focused upon in this article are also most reflective of a particular pattern of lesbian life, where identification as a lesbian occurs in the transition to adulthood, without prior long-term heterosexual involvement or children from such involvement; the young adult years are marked by engagement in lesbian community and multiple lesbian relationships; and as the era of young adulthood ends and midlife begins, issues arise related to the establishment and maintenance of a long-term committed relationship and the decision to raise children. By focusing on this one pattern of lesbian life, individual differences in relationship and family circumstance, coming-out histories, and the meanings attached to claiming a lesbian sexual identity are, along with race, ethnicity, socioeconomic backgrounds, gender identities, and physical appearance and abilities, of necessity glossed over. Yet such differences likely impact conceptions and constructions of lesbians' friendships. The patterns described in this article are offered as a beginning for more closely considering just how some lesbians at midlife today from one particular background may conceptualize and experience friendships.

LESBIANS AT MIDLIFE

To understand midlife lesbians' friendships, it is important to first consider midlife itself as experienced by lesbians. Although more and more heterosexual women may be choosing to remain child-free, the midlife structure for white heterosexual women typically has been organized around reproduction and child rearing; these organizational structures continue to dominate both the lives and the societal images of women at midlife (Gergen, 1990; Levinson, 1996). Yet these structures are less pervasive as organizing frameworks for lesbians (Kirkpatrick, 1989). This is not to say that midlife lesbians are not engaged in reproduction and child rearing. Indeed, some are raising children borne in the context of relationships with men during young adulthood. Furthermore, midlife as well as young adult lesbians today are increasingly choosing to have and raise children as out lesbians–and typically with life partners (for more on lesbians as parents and lesbian families, see, e.g., Demo & Allen, 1996; Laird, 1993; Patterson, 1995b; Slater, 1995). But lesbian culture does not itself center on these activities. While the culture is adapting to incorporate these realities of lesbians' lives, that culture also includes attention to political activism, lesbian community, and lesbian friendships. Indeed, as Lewin (1996) argues, lesbians often seek to consciously highlight in their commitment ceremonies their resistance as well as accommodation to marriage and norms of heterosexuality. While children are becoming more a part of lesbians' lives through a diversity of pathways and across a wide range of ages, there remains to date great variability in the extent to which children are present in the lives of midlife lesbians, and in the roles that they play.

There is also variability among lesbians with regard to participation in long-term romantic partner relationships. Yet such a relationship–be it real or desired–may be the most common organizing structure for midlife lesbians today. Rothblum, Mintz, Cowan, and Haller (1995) point out that lesbians at midlife typically are in–or striving for–long-term partnerships. It seems that many, if not most, adult lesbians anticipate growing old with a partner (Bell & Weinberg, 1978; Blumstein & Schwartz, 1983; Bryant & Demian, 1994; Kurdek, 1995; Loulan, 1991; Peplau, 1993; Saghir & Robins, 1973; Savin-Williams, 1995; Slater, 1995; Tully, 1989). As Rose (1996) argues, the dominant cultural script for lesbians is the romance script–lesbians move through courtship towards the goal of establishing a permanent relationship. The predominant script for lesbians, as for heterosexual women, appears to be a couple relationship that continues as a long-term partnership. The extent to which alternative patterns of relationships are accepted and respected varies across lesbian communities and friendship groups. Many who study and theorize about lesbians' families note that alternative family forms do exist; still, most if not all of their attention is on those families comprising a monogamous partner and now, increasingly, children.

Midlife may be a particularly significant time for lesbians' family development in a context of heterosexism. Heterosexism alters lesbians' individual and family life cycles (see, e.g., Kimmel & Sang, 1995; Kurdek, 1995; Reid, 1995; Slater, 1995; Slater & Mencher, 1991), not only by limiting lesbians' rights to raise children, but also by not recognizing, validating, and supporting lesbian romantic partnerships and long-term commitments. At midlife, however, lesbian identity may have more room to maneuver and lesbians' lovers may gain a different status (Loulan, 1991). There may be a decrease in efforts on the part of parents to change a child in midlife compared to young adulthood; there may also be more acceptance of a child's sexuality as parents recognize, finally, that it is not just a phase (Rothblum et al., 1995). Due to ageism, there is also a decreased likelihood that people will look at a midlife lesbian couple and think about sex. This, combined with the years of familiarity one's family of origin may have with a lesbian's long-term partner, may make the relationship more acceptable and accepted. Alternatively, for those lesbians beginning a new relationship at midlife, Loulan (1991) suggests that families of origin simply may be happy to see that their daughter is no longer alone. In other words, at midlife, one's family of origin may be more used to and accepting of the idea of their daughter as a lesbian. The introduction of children also may bring families of origin back into the picture and even may help to reduce their heterosexism (see Patterson, 1996; see also Slater, 1995).

Renewed or strengthened connections with families of origin may be validating for lesbians, particularly those who are engaged in partner relationships and parenting activities that reflect closely the norms of their families of origin (besides the difference in sexual identities). But these connections–and the expectations that may go with them–may be problematic for midlife lesbians who bring different values and structures to their relationships and who are seeking to create alternative family forms that do not easily fit into the family forms their families of origin wish to validate. Similarly, for lesbians who share many values with their families of origin, it still may be that to remain in or be able to return to these families, lesbians have to follow certain rules and patterns of behavior that may not be good for their individual health and development, nor for their partner relationships and families of creation (Brown, 1995; see also Brosnan, 1996). For example, Brown (1995) notes that some lesbians may be asked to remain closeted in their families of origin, at least to some members; or perhaps they may be known as lesbians and thus expected to be grateful for being allowed to continue to participate in family events with their partners–as long as they are not affectionate in front of anyone. Judy MacLean (1995, p. 23) reflects the question Brown (1995) is raising when she says, "As a lesbian, I've been so busy trying to get *into* the family circle that I forgot to ask whether I would be interested in what goes on inside it." There may be a great trade-off with respect to emotional health and validation of their own families of creation for some lesbians who seek to remain in–or return to–their families of origin; there also may be a great trade-off with respect to time and energy for friendships–a point further explored shortly. These tensions may become more evident–and more in need of re-examination–at midlife.

For those lesbians who reach midlife after living as lesbians through young adulthood, the process of self-development may be more continual than for heterosexual women at midlife who have followed a traditional life course. It also may involve a wider range of options for healthy, successful adulthood and aging. Indeed, while many developmental theories and the larger society may posit marriage and parenting as the markers of true adulthood or at least well-being (Demo & Allen, 1996; Smolak, 1993), lesbians at midlife are likely to have discovered for themselves their own ways of entering into and moving through adulthood that may or may not include–and are less likely to be restricted only to–the roles of partner and parent.

In addition to heterosexist models of development, lesbians at midlife also face, along with heterosexual and bisexual women, the stigma of aging that predominates in an ageist society. This stigma may be more shocking to white heterosexuals than to white lesbians, lesbians of color, and heterosexual women of color, because the latter groups are more likely to have had to deal with and adjust to societal stigma by the time they reach midlife. Furthermore, growing older for lesbians may provide greater freedom for being out as lesbians, less pressure to date men, and/or less of a need to live a double life (Kirkpatrick, 1989; Loulan, 1991). Indeed, lesbians at midlife and old age may find themselves free of the pressures to marry and to parent–either because others have stopped putting on the pressure or because they have come to recognize that these are not the only markers for healthy adulthood. On the other hand, there may be added concerns that health care providers and retirement options may be inadequate to meet the needs of lesbians (Tully, 1989). This may be of particular concern to lesbians who have not raised children, who are not in partner relationships, and/or who have not remained a part of their families of origin. But it also may, for these women, highlight and reinforce the importance of friendships.

Lesbians enter and move through midlife in a diversity of contexts. Some may be in long-term partnerships, others may be newly partnered or newly single, and still others may choose to be single. Among these, some may have children from prior heterosexual relationships, from a currently ongoing lesbian relationship, or from a prior lesbian relationship that is ongoing as friends and co-parents. Furthermore, relationships with families of origin may have been severed for years; while for others, relationships may be ongoing, but there is either no knowledge or limited acceptance of the lesbian's identity or family of creation. Additionally, some lesbians at midlife may find themselves drawn back to the family of origin because of the needs of aging parents or their desires to connect with their nieces and nephews; similarly, families of origin may find themselves seeking to reconnect or improve connections with their lesbian family members for the same reasons. Along with the historical changes described earlier in this paper, each of these contexts shapes the midlife experience in particular ways. Each also shapes the manner in which friendships at midlife are imagined and conducted.

LESBIANS' FRIENDSHIPS

Only a very few researchers have concentrated their research attention on examining lesbians' experiences in and perspectives on friendships (see, e.g., Hall & Rose, 1996; Nardi & Sherrod, 1994; O'Boyle & Thomas, 1996; Stanley, 1996; see also Weinstock, in press, for a review). Relatively speaking, there is more published theorizing and personal reflections (see, e.g., Card, 1995; Daly, 1996; Hoagland, 1988, 1992; Kitzinger, 1996; Kitzinger & Perkins, 1993; Nardi & Sherrod, 1994; Raymond, 1986, 1990; Weinstock & Rothblum, 1996a, 1996b). Supplementing the limited availability of direct, explicit research and reflection upon lesbians' friendships, much of what we know about lesbians' friendships has been gleaned from studies focused on other issues related to lesbians' experiences–for example, lesbians' experiences with partners, families of origin, and children (see, e.g., Hetrick & Martin, 1987; Kurdek, 1988, 1995; Kurdek & Schmitt, 1987; Lewin, 1993);

lesbians' and bisexual women's attitudes towards bisexuality and bisexual women (Rust, 1995); historical examinations of various lesbian communities (see, e.g., Faderman, 1991; Kennedy & Davis; 1993); and examinations of lesbians' mental, emotional, and social supports (see, e.g., D'Augelli, 1989b; D'Augelli, Collins, & Hart, 1987). Furthermore, the focus of available research and theorizing about lesbians' lives in general and lesbians' friendships in particular has typically been on young adult women with race, education, and economic privilege who self-identify as lesbians and who are participants in established gay and lesbian activities and organizations. Most studies also have been based on relatively small samples.

One theme that has received attention is *sexual tensions in lesbians' friendships*; while sometimes explored from a political perspective–the role of sex in friendships might be examined, as Esther Rothblum does (see also Rothblum, 1994; Rothblum & Brehony, 1993), in a manner that seeks to expand or alter the meaning of friends and lovers, sex and sexual activity–oftentimes explorations of such issues involve consideration of lesbians' friendships as they may impact upon lesbians' lover relationships. For example, friendships as precursors to lover relationships and/or as alternatives to such relationships have been considered (e.g., Rose, 1996; Rose, Zand, & Cini, 1993; Rothblum & Brehony, 1993; Vetere, 1982). But more often, attention has been paid to the role of friends as validators and supports for lesbian couple relationships or, conversely, as threats to or possible distractions from the demands (e.g., time and attention) and/or difficulties of such relationships (see, e.g., Clunis & Greene, 1988; Kurdek, 1988; Slater, 1994; Stanley, 1996). The tendencies for many lesbians to consider their lovers to be their best friends and to remain friends with ex-lovers also have been frequently highlighted (e.g., Clunis & Greene, 1988; Peplau, 1993) and occasionally researched (e.g., Becker, 1988; Stanley, 1996). Some attention has been paid as well to the presence and qualities of lesbians' friendships with heterosexual (e.g., O'Boyle & Thomas, 1996; Palladino & Stephenson, 1990) and bisexual (e.g., Bond & Weinstock, in press; Rust, 1995) women.

By far, as with heterosexual friendships, the theme that has received the greatest empirical attention has been that of *describing* lesbians' friendships–particularly with whom lesbians are friends–and *identifying* the roles friends play in supporting lesbians' individual health and development (see, e.g., Bradford, Ryan, & Rothblum, 1994; D'Augelli &

Hart, 1987; Grana, 1989; Kurdek & Schmitt, 1987). Lesbians, like their heterosexual counterparts (see, e.g., Blieszner & Adams, 1992; O'Connor, 1992), tend to be friends with similar others on a multiplicity of dimensions, including race, age, sex, socioeconomic class, current rela tionship circumstance, and sexuality (see Weinstock, in press, for a review). That is, while there are exceptions, lesbians tend to be friends with other lesbians like themselves (see, e.g., D'Augelli, 1989a; Rust, 1995).

As for the roles friends play in lesbians' lives, most research has concentrated on exploring the roles of friends in fostering lesbians' psychosocial and social well-being. Much less attention has been paid to friends' roles in fostering the development of lesbian communities, feminist alliances, or other political actions. Drawing upon what has been studied, it does appear that friendships for lesbians are typically positive sources of both support and satisfaction; they also appear to play an important role in lesbians' positive experiences of themselves as lesbians (see, e.g., D'Augelli, 1989a; D'Augelli & Hart, 1987; D'Augelli et al., 1987; Stanley, 1996; see Weinstock, in press, for a review). Furthermore, friends have been identified as important in the process of lesbians' claiming and sustaining a positive lesbian identity.

Friends as family. In the 1970s, a time when the modern lesbian, gay, bisexual and transgender movements were emerging in the United States, LGBT people were defined–and oftentimes came to define themselves–as outside the family, indeed, antithetical to family. LGBT people were viewed as uninterested in and incapable of family relationships. While privately, LGBT people formed their own families, these were typically hidden from public view, as were LGBT identities themselves. But the last few decades have evidenced a rise in public attention to families by LGBT persons who began to claim their rights to families of creation in part by using the language of "family" in general and "families of choice" and "friends as family" in particular to highlight the existence and importance of families to LGBT people. The use of this language helped to shift both private and public images of LGBT persons as somehow separate from families. Indeed, the act of naming family as composed of chosen members–including friends–was a powerful personal and political strategy for LGBT persons (see Weston, 1991; see also Nardi, 1992). Today, these phrases are familiar; a diversity of researchers, theorists, and social service providers have noted the tendency for LGBT persons to rely upon their friends in ways that heterosexuals typically rely upon traditional family members (see, e.g., Friend, 1989; Nardi, 1992; Weston, 1991). For example, Nardi (1992) noted that lesbians' and gay men's friends are a form of family, and Kimmel (1992, p. 38) identified three roles that gay men and lesbians can play in families: (a) long-term partners; (b) caretakers, financial supporters, and other special roles in families of origin, due to their presumably "single" status and/or lesser likelihood of being a part of a traditional family of creation; and (c) members of "self-created networks of friends, significant others, and selected biological family members that provide mutual support of various kinds, as family systems might do." Similarly, several writers (e.g., Kus, 1991; Laird, 1993; Nardi, 1982; Shernoff, 1984; Weston, 1991) have argued that therapists, theorists, and/or researchers ought to expand the traditional meaning of "family" to include non-traditional important others. That is, these authors argue, in the course of theorizing, research, therapy, and other work with lesbian and gay clients, that it is important to include current friendship families.

Little is known, however, about the extent of–and reasons for–conceptualizing and creating friends as family among individual LGBT persons today. The construct itself may have developed among LGBT people in response to their anticipated and/or real exclusion from their families of origin (see Weston, 1991, 1996), as well as limited legitimization and support for families of creation with partners and children (see Patterson & Redding, 1996). But most of the theorizing and research on lesbians' friends and families has focused on young adulthood and on previous historical contexts. In the remainder of this article, I consider lesbians' friendships at midlife today, with particular attention to the ways that historical context and developmental period may interact in the construction and prevalence of one of three conceptualizations of friends as family.

LESBIANS' FRIENDS AT MIDLIFE

Given the limited attention paid to date to midlife lesbians and to lesbians' friendships in general, it is not surprising that research on and theorizing about lesbians' friendships at midlife also is quite limited. Drawing upon what is available, including published personal reflections and the small sample of interviews I have conducted as part of my ongoing study of midlife lesbians' friendships, it does appear that friendships play an important role in the lives of midlife lesbians today. In an exploratory study by Tully (1989) of a sample comprising mostly white, professional, midlife lesbians, respondents reported high involvement with friendship networks; they also noted that women friends were especially likely to provide caregiving support: "women relatives (N – 38, 52%) and, more specifically, women friends (N = 65, 89%) were identified as the ones from whom these midlife lesbians sought and received the most support" (Tully, 1989, pp. 96-97). These women also reported that they turned first to their lovers or emotionally close women friends for caregiving, and that emotional support and personal care from other women as well as ongoing companionship from other women–especially from lesbians their own age–were "vitally necessary" (p. 97). In addition, Kirkpatrick suggests that the high value lesbians place on intimacy "fuels and helps maintain the supportive network of friendships characteristic of many older lesbians" (Wolf, 1978, in Kirkpatrick, 1989, p. 141). Furthermore, in their review of midlife lesbians' relationships, Kimmel and Sang (1995, p. 197) note that both single midlife women and those who are partnered "tended to derive support and a sense of connection from friends, family, and the lesbian community." They also tended to spend their social time with and receive support from other lesbians their own age–including lovers, ex-lovers, and friends–or to engage in mixed lesbian and gay activities (see, e.g., Bradford & Ryan, 1988, 1991; Sang, 1991). Strikingly, in Sang's (1991) questionnaire study of 110 midlife lesbians, 38% of the respondents noted that they derived both meaning and satisfaction from their friendships, 47% from their intimate relationships, and 12% from their children. While there were additional categories of responses, other family relationships were not identified.

The tendency for lesbians to maintain ties–and often close friendship ties–with ex-lovers as well as the larger lesbian community has been noted frequently (see, e.g., Becker, 1988; Kirkpatrick, 1989; Rothblum et al., 1995). Rothblum et al. (1995, p. 68) note that midlife may bring with it "a renewed sense of the importance of friends." This may be particularly true among those lesbians who do not have the support of their families of origin, and those who currently have or anticipate an increased need for caregiving support due to their physical health; because of heterosexism, lesbians may not anticipate finding sufficient support from formal caregiving service systems (see, e.g., Bradford & Ryan, 1991; Pred, 1986/1996; Tully, 1989). Similarly, Kirkpatrick (1989, p. 141), reflecting on lesbians in middle adulthood, noted that "lesbians tend to have a close network of friends which may substitute for estranged family and kin." Close friendship ties may be especially likely when lesbians are not out to their families of origin or when these families react negatively to their daughters' lesbian identity (Lipman, 1986). The importance of friendship networks frequently has been identified as one consequence of heterosexism (see, e.g., Kimmel, 1992; Kurdek & Schmitt, 1986; Lipman, 1986; Raphael & Robinson, 1984). Indeed, the first meaning of friends as family, described next, closely reflects this context of heterosexism.

1. *Friends as substitute family members.* Many lesbians in midlife today came out in a context in which lesbianism was constructed as a deviant identity, and being a lesbian meant that one would not be accepted in one's family of origin nor likely be supported in forming long-term romantic partnerships or relationships with children. In such a context, friendships might be expected to hold tremendous importance. Indeed, friends may have been the only family some of the lesbians of this era were able to form and sustain. A diversity of individual lesbians, empirical researchers, theorists, and social service providers who work with lesbians (see, e.g., Kirkpatrick, 1989; Kurdek, 1988; Weston, 1991) have emphasized the role of friends as substitute family members. Consider, for example, the conclusion offered by Nardi and Sherrod, after conducting their questionnaire study of lesbians' and gay men's friendships; they wrote: "friends provide gay people with an identity and a source of social support that are not often available in a heterosexual, sometimes hostile culture (Nardi & Sherrod, 1994, p. 197). In an earlier work, Nardi (1982) argued that one way to conceptualize lesbian and gay "families" is as an extended family of close gay friends. Nardi also noted the likelihood of such a family developing as a consequence of being gay in a heterosexual world. This actually leads gay men and lesbians to form a network of close gay and lesbian friends; it is these friends who help the gay or lesbian person develop and maintain a positive gay or lesbian identity. Thus, in contrast to a network of close heterosexual friends, the gay network of friends/family:

> arises out of a need to find role models and identity in an oppressive society. The heterosexual friendship group for heterosexuals may be close and important, but it occurs as an option in the

context of a heterosexually dominant society. However, the gay person must create, out of necessity, a meaningful friendship group to cope with threats to identity and self-esteem in a world of heterosexual work situations, traditional family systems, and stereotyped media images. (Nardi, 1982, p. 86)

Carol, a white lesbian in her 50s whom I interviewed, reflected a similar theme when she said:

I think friendships are particularly important in the lesbian and gay community because I think oftentimes families do reject [us]. Or they may not; they verbally say they accept, [but] there is a lot of tension. And so I think extended family is particularly important in the lesbian and gay community.

Asked what she means by extended family, she goes on:

I mean just really close friends who can be really supportive and almost be as family members, as blood relatives would be in situations of crisis and whatever. I think it's particularly important in our community to have those friendships.

Another white lesbian, Rosemary, in her early 40s, explicitly notes the replacement role friends play as family because of not being as secure in her family of origin:

You know, if I was to say who my best friends are right now, it would be my partner, it would be my ex-partner. I mean, if I had to categorize friends, those are my best friends in the whole wide world, and they know more about me than anybody else knows about me. So friendships have played an important part in my life, and friends are important to me. And more important to me now, because of family relationships not being as solid as they have been in the past. So kind of doing what I, I guess we call in the gay, lesbian, bisexual, transgender community, the family of choice versus the family of origin.

The approach reflected in these comments, and much of the research, theoretical, and autobiographical literature, involves viewing friends from the perspective of substitute family members–replacements for the loss of access to or support from traditional families of origin, and/or limited opportunities and supports for creating families with partners and children. While it is certainly a political act for lesbians to claim and create families of their own, whatever the underlying motivation or need, the conceptualization of "friends as family" just described appears to emerge from and reflect the limited support lesbians may receive from family, and thus their greater need for friends to fulfill traditional family functions (e.g., D'Augelli, 1989b; D'Augelli et al., 1987; Grana, 1989; Weston, 1991). This construction of friends as family may have emerged from and most closely reflects the prior, pre-gay liberation, pre-feminist historical era, when most if not all lesbians had to be closeted and lesbians themselves were conceptualized as unacceptable members of families of origin as well as families of creation with partners and children. It also may most closely reflect the developmental time period that involves initial separation from family of origin, entry into adulthood, and the claiming of a lesbian identity. Yet this pattern has relevance for midlife lesbians today, particularly those who continue to be rejected by or isolated from their families of origin and extended family members who do not know, understand, or accept them as lesbians, and/or those who are not partnered and raising children. Even as these lesbians may continue or renew their connections with their families of origin, their friendships and, for those who are partnered, their partners may be what sustains them and functions like family in their day-to-day lives.

Indeed, among those midlife lesbians with partners, friends may be specifically experienced as substitute extended family members, while one's partner is viewed and experienced as immediate family. For some lesbians at midlife, making such a distinction may be particularly important as a means of sustaining and supporting their romantic partner relationship. For example, Carol, introduced earlier, said, when asked who her closest friend is:

> Beth [her partner] is my closest friend. . . . I suppose that may not always be true for people, but certainly without question she is my dearest and closest friend, in addition to being my partner. All of those things that I mentioned that identify close friends are double pluses for her. It would be very hard for me to name anybody that even came close. . . . I think for me it's probably a matter of degree. The degree to which I have those things with

Beth, I don't think I could ever have with anybody else. Some of those things are present with other people. I think I have some really fine friends who are very caring, who are good listeners, who have the same kinds of feelings that I do about a number of issues, who like some of the same kinds of things that I do, but it's a matter of degree I think. I just really don't feel that I have another friend that even comes close.

Carol also talks about and distinguishes between friendships formed as a couple and friendships that one member of a couple forms with a single woman. The latter, she notes, might be weird; it is better to have couple friends because, she says:

. . . if one of the people starts to form a strong friendship with somebody outside of the relationship, if that strong friendship is formed with somebody who's free and single, then there's doubt on the partner's part about what that relationship really is. Whereas if the two of you are forming a relationship with two other people who have a stable relationship, then there is no jealousy, no concern about what is really going on here. So sure, I think it's easier for a couple to form a relationship with another couple.

Similarly, Fran, another white woman in her 40s whom I interviewed, noted that after having an affair with one of her friends, at a time when she and her long-term partner were having problems, she is more careful about the friendships she develops. She doesn't want to become attracted to a friend again, or have a friend attracted to her because, as she puts it, "my relationship with Andrea [partner] is too important to me to allow anything to interfere with that." Like Carol, she considers her partner to be her best friend as well as her partner. Other friends are clearly important, but they function more as substitutes for extended family members than as immediate family. And there is a clear line between partner/best friend and other friends. Similarly, for both Fran and Carol, they remain in touch with their ex-lovers, and some of these are friends, but they are not close friends.

2. *Friends as a challenge to the core structure of the family.* In the above conceptualization of friends as family, the emphasis is on choosing and developing family relationships with friends, especially as substitutes for extended family members. The structure or concept of the family itself is not identified as problematic. In contrast, some

lesbian activists, researchers, and theorists have focused on friends as family specifically as a challenge to the nuclear structure of the family (see, e.g., Brosnan, 1996; Jo, 1996). There are several challenges that friends might pose to the family structure; the one I focus on here involves a challenge to the centering of one's partner in favor of the creation of families based on shared political as well as personal commitments to other lesbians. This challenge frequently involves–or implies–the placement of lesbians' friendships rather than lesbians' lover relationships at the center of family life. "Friends as family," from this perspective, represents a challenge to the organizing structure of the modern Euro-American traditional nuclear family, based as it is on a primary, sexual, and romantic partnership between two adults.

Some theorists and activists who pose this challenge actually reject the phrasing of "friends as family" because they see it as continuing to center and privilege both the family and heterosexuality (see, e.g., Jo, 1996; Weston, 1991; see Weinstock, in press, for a review). By naming family, it keeps our attention on family, and it also treats family as something to which friends ought to aspire. In contrast, these writers are more interested in centering friends and claiming the specialness and importance of friends–not as family–but as friends. They focus on identifying and considering the personal and political challenges that arise when friendships are placed at the center of lesbians' lives (e.g., Card, 1995; Kitzinger, 1996; Kitzinger & Perkins, 1993; Strega, 1996). At the same time, there is a push to honor our friendships by developing our own terminology to describe our distinct experiences in these relationships (see, e.g., Jo, 1996; Weston, 1991). While these women reject the phrase "friends as family," they share with those who rely upon it the goal of building lesbian friendships and community and breaking away from the privileging of lover and family relationships over friendships.

This pattern of friendship seems to most closely reflect the era of lesbian feminism, when lesbians' allegiances were more likely to other lesbians and to lesbian community, and not (yet) to a specific partner and the raising of children, and there were limited expectations for relationship longevity. This pattern also may reflect the developmental period of young adulthood, especially the 20s. Still, it is a pattern that continues in the lives of some lesbians today (see, e.g., Jo, 1996; Strega, 1996) who seek to "create our own culture of love and closeness and commitment" (Jo, 1996, p. 290) and who view lesbian friendships as "the building blocks of lesbian communities and politics" (Kitzinger, 1996, p. 298; see also Card, 1995). It also exists among some lesbians who place equal-or greater-value on friendships than on couple relationships (see Rose, 1996; Weinstock & Rothblum, 1996a). For example, Elizabeth, a white lesbian in her 30s, in a fairly new romantic relationship, had this exchange during my interview with her:

> . . . I still see my primary support system as my friendship network, more so than my relationship. IS YOUR SENSE THAT THAT WILL CHANGE OVER TIME IF THE RELATIONSHIP CONTINUES, OR . . . ? I think they will probably become equal, I would hope so, but I don't see it superseding my relationships with my friends.

Furthermore, when asked what her ideal for herself was around family, she had this to say:

> I've got a T-shirt somewhere that says, you know, "a family is a circle of friends that loves you." I love that. And I guess by and large that's on target for me.

It is important to note that Elizabeth is not currently in a committed, long-term partner relationship, nor has she yet entered midlife. It is possible that she will sustain her commitment to the centrality of friendships even as she enters midlife and even in the context of a long-term partner relationship. Yet it is also possible that, as both contexts change, Elizabeth may find herself, like other midlife lesbians, prioritizing her romantic partnership. Indeed, Elizabeth anticipates this occurrence when she continues to describe her ideal for herself around family in the following manner:

> I would like to have a significant relationship, a long-term relationship with someone, which would, in my mind, sort of constitute my real, sort of primary family. And sort of see very closely around that long-term friends with whom I've got a lot of shared history and connection and that I would share holidays and significant times and events with. And some of those people might be blood relationships or family of origin, or whatever we want

to call those, and some of those are, are friends of real significance and depth and substance.

For Elizabeth, then, friends are currently her primary supports, and she anticipates they will continue to be central. Yet when envisioning a significant, long-term relationship, she continues to view friends as very close and significant, but she also appears to view them as "very closely around" the partner relationship but not exactly part of her "real, sort of primary family." With this statement, Elizabeth begins to appear not to be challenging the centrality of lover relationships as much as seeking to sustain their centrality and the centrality of her friendships; this idea begins to reflect a third way of thinking about "friends as family," described shortly.

Kath Weston (1991), in a participant observation and in-depth interview study with lesbians and gay men, also identified similar conceptions of "families we choose." Most of her interviewees spoke of building families of friends as a political challenge to the family as we know it, especially the centrality and privileging of biological ties and heterosexuality. A small minority of her sample reflected the perspective that friends as family was really a substitute for unavailable family forms, an alternative borne of oppression rather than a revolutionary challenge to the status quo. For these individuals, like the "friends as substitute family" pattern already described, lesbians and gay men "choose" and "create" families of friends not because they seek to challenge the status quo, but because the status quo has historically denied and/or limited their family possibilities (see also Weston, 1996). In a context of oppression, this is both a political as well as a personal feat.

3. *Friends as in-laws: Negotiating a place in between friends and lovers.* The question arises: What will become of the notion of "friends as family" as lesbians are no longer viewed as or view themselves as antithetical to family, and as "family" issues are claimed as part of lesbians' political and personal agendas? Today, young adult and midlife lesbians are increasingly having and co-parenting children with romantic partners, domestic partnerships and other supports for partner relationships are becoming more available, and legal marriage appears a possibility. While these movements into the mainstream indicate progress, it is important to consider the potential losses as well. Specifically, as more and more lesbians construct pro-

creational families, and are less marginalized by their families of origin and society as a whole, what might happen to their ways of conceptualizing families and friendships? Will there be less of an impetus for lesbians to build lesbian friendship families and communities?

It does appear that there is, now, less of a need for friends to serve as substitutes for families, and that there is also less of a political push by lesbians in general to develop alternative family forms based on friendships rather than romantic partnerships. However, friends themselves continue to hold great value; this valuation of friendships may be reflected in a third way of conceptualizing friends as family that does not appear to be articulated in the literature to date. Indeed, it may be more observable now that midlife lesbians are increasingly and publically in romantic partner relationships and/or raising children, and are seeking to negotiate their own ways of balancing the multiple demands, responsibilities, and desires of this time period. Specifically, some lesbians who speak of their friends as family appear to be seeking to negotiate a place in between a challenge to the core, central adult relationship that typically organizes families–the lover relationship–and the temporary substitute value of friends when this relationship and/or supportive family of origin relationships are unavailable. These lesbians appear to view a partner/lover relationship as "primary," yet at the same time they wish to sustain their intimate and in some ways also primary friendships. Indeed, it appears that "friends as family" may be a means for lesbians at midlife to negotiate having both a partner and close friends with whom one is very intimate. It may be a means by which midlife lesbians negotiate the feelings of jealousy, insecurity, and the sense of being left out that both a lover and close friends may feel. It may be a means as well for lesbians to negotiate sexual feelings, attractions, and tensions among friends and lovers. Indeed, "friends as family" may be a strategy that enables lesbians to negotiate sexual tensions in friendships and, more broadly, to negotiate multiple, close, intimate relationships–only one of which is likely to be genitally sexual, but all of which are passionately experienced.

In explaining this way of viewing "friends as family," it is important to mention the tendency, noted in the literature and among my small sample, for lesbians with partners to view these partners as their closest friends and for those who do not currently have but who desire partners to envision these partners being their closest friends. Furthermore, there is a tendency for lesbians to wish to remain friends with their ex-lovers (see, e.g., Becker, 1988; Hite, 1987; Nardi & Sherrod, 1994; Slater, 1995; Stanley, 1996). Also important to mention is that a common pattern by which lesbians become lovers is through friendship (the friendship script; see Rose et al., 1993; see also Grammick, 1984; Vetere, 1982). For example, Fran, introduced earlier, noted that she and her long-term partner were friends before becoming involved in their romantic relationship, and that they remain friends. Indeed, as she put it, "Thinking of my partner not being my best friend is something that doesn't compute. . . . I wouldn't want it any other way." The course of development from friends to lovers, however, is not necessarily a clear one; these two forms of relationships are themselves intertwined for many lesbians (see, e.g., Diamond, 1996, in Diamond, 1997; Futcher & Hutchins, 1996; Munson, 1996; Vetere, 1982).

For lesbians at midlife, there may be an increased need or desire to reexamine and reorganize the balance constructed among one's commitments, including to a lover and to friends, as well as to one's family of origin and the larger community. Most of the available literature on midlife, and the transition to midlife, suggests this is a time for reorganizing important aspects of one's life and the self (see, e.g., Levinson, 1978, 1996; Stewart & Gold-Steinberg, 1990), often motivated by a new awareness of one's location in the life course and one's relationship to the aging process. For some current midlife lesbians, it also may be a time of return to, as well as reconciliation with, one's family of origin. Some midlife lesbians' parents may require caretaking as they age; some siblings and parents may make renewed attempts to learn about and understand the lesbian's life and identity; and some siblings may recognize their desire for their own children to know their aunts. Additionally, some lesbians may make renewed efforts to be a part of their families of origin, and to be known and accepted as lesbians within them. And for some midlife lesbians, this may be just the time they adopt or bear children of their own, while others may be focusing on building–or changing–careers. With all these possibilities–and realities–coupled with the changing perspective often brought about by the recognition of one's midlife location itself, there may be an increased need to reconsider priorities as well as to alter or resolve long-standing patterns or issues so as to make room for new desires and life balances.

The extent to which one effects or responds to changes in the midlife structure by shifting priorities among friends, partners, families of origin, children, and careers depends on a diversity of factors. Yet the practical need for negotiating among multiple relationships at this busy time of life cannot be overstated. What I turn to now is describing a particular kind of balance that midlife lesbians may strike among the multiple relationships in their lives–one that seeks to find a way to center both a partner and close friends.

Rosemary, a white lesbian in her 40s, spoke during an interview I conducted with her about the struggle to negotiate her continued connection with her ex-partner, her own relationship with her partner, and her ex-partner's current lover relationship. For Rosemary, the struggle is twofold (at least). On the one hand, Rosemary has had to work with her current partner to help her partner accept and honor the relationship she has with her former partner; similarly, her ex-partner has to work with her new partner to accept their ex-lover, friendship relationship. As Rosemary put it, her ex-partner's current partner "doesn't know quite what to do with me or our relationship." She goes on:

> [My ex-lover, Helen] is still a very important part of my life, but she has a partner in her life now, and, you know, her partner is very resentful and jealous of me and doesn't understand how we can still be in this relationship. And we understand that, but it's kind of like, you know, you get Helen, you get a package deal because you get Rosemary along. And if you get Rosemary, you get a package deal because you get Helen along with it.

And, with respect to her own current relationship, she notes that:

> calling my ex-partner my best friend, that was a real struggle for my present partner, not understanding that. Like, where does best friends stop and where does previous partner, you know. And we have not been sexually involved with each other at all. If you ask me if I love Helen, I love her dearly. And so, you know, it sounds like a fine line but it's a very clear line for me, very clear line for [Helen], and, and Mary, my present partner is as much my best friend, and probably more, you know.

This example does not easily fit into the two conceptualizations of friends as family described thus far and typically offered by lesbian friendship researchers, theorists, and service providers. Rosemary appears to be engaged in an effort to negotiate the centrality of friendship relationships–in this case an ex-lover friendship–in a way that keeps a "very clear line" between friend and partner and at the same time blurs the line in certain respects. Indeed, the negotiation seems to involve an effort to hold her partner as central at the same time as recognizing and holding firm to the importance and in some manner centrality of close friendships. What I suggest here is that "friends as family" may in fact be a strategy by which lesbians in committed, monogamous relationships at midlife make close, intimate friendships feel safer to their current partners, their friends' current partners, and to themselves, than they might be if they remained conceptualized as friends but not family.

More broadly speaking, "friends as family" may be a strategy by which lesbians at midlife create and negotiate their own type of in-law relationships, where in-laws are friends rather than biological family. As family, these friends come with a lesbian into a new romantic relationship, and remain a part of the family over time. Furthermore, as family, those friends who were previously romantic partners or who currently involve sexual attraction need not be a threat (or as much of a threat) to partner relationships. Reliance upon the notion of family–particularly a notion of family that makes room for a special and unique place for both partners and close friends–helps to place a friend more clearly and firmly outside the realm of possible romantic interest but inside the family. And, over the continued course of a romantic partnership, it also helps each lesbian keep her friends on her own "side" of the family, at the same time as it provides added impetus to acknowledge and–with more or less success–accept the partner's friends as part of the family.

This same strategy for negotiating boundaries between friends and lovers may prove useful for a diversity of friendships, including those among single lesbians, and those where there is little sexual interest but great emotional attachment, as well as friendships where both sexual and emotional interest are present. As an example, Jan, a white lesbian in her late 30s who describes herself as "approaching 40," is not currently in a partner relationship. During my interview with her, Jan noted that one of her two closest friends is someone for whom she has strong emotional feelings, and for whom she has had sexual feelings and attractions as well. She describes her current way of thinking about this friendship as:

> like us being sisters, in a blood sense. That, she is to me, like a sister, I mean, you know we confide in each other, we cry together, we laugh together, we do things that sisters would do, and we know just about everything about each other.

Jan explains that this conception of close friends as sisters emerged from her struggle to make sense of her strong feelings for her friend, including her sexual feelings, which were not reciprocated to a similar degree. As Jan put it, conceptualizing this friend as a sister has "been helpful in separating the sexual part out in a healthy way." As sisters, she feels she will be less able and willing to view the friendship in anything other than friendship terms. At the same time, the reference to sister, to this friend as family, helps Jan to feel assured of "the depth of commitment to the relationship." As she put it,

> A sister is someone who really stays there through it all. Whereas a friend can come and go, they may blow me off, you know, if they just don't have the energy, or they're just not as invested.

It is this meaning of friends as family that has not typically been attended to in the research or theoretical literature–as a strategy for negotiating undesired sexual feelings, jealousy, and possessiveness in lesbians' friendships. That this is a strategy used by some lesbians in negotiating friendships is not surprising given that the most frequently mentioned concern raised by the lesbians who participated in Jeanne Stanley's (1996, p. 53) focus group research was "the potential threat of a friend becoming romantically involved with one member of the couple." Naming friends as family may be a strategy lesbians use to sustain important friendships, including ex-lover friendships; it may ease one's own and one's partner's concerns about the closeness of these relationships at the same time as it creates a structure within which such friendships are recognized as part of one's family that comes along into any new family form. It may not be easy to negotiate these in-law relationships, but as Rosemary put it, "it's a package deal." If you get her, you get her ex-lover; that is what happens with in-laws.

To summarize, "friends as family" may reflect a strategy lesbians use to make a place at the family table for both friends and lovers, a place that recognizes the importance and centrality of both forms of relationships and that seeks to negotiate the tensions that arise or may arise between these relationship forms, or within ourselves in relation to these relationships. Sometimes, of course, these negotiations do not work, and lesbians give up or withdraw some intimacy from friendships to preserve partner relationships; at times, the reverse occurs. Yet it may be that "friends as family" is a concept that provides a framework that pushes current partners to work harder than they might like at times to find a place for their partners' close friends in their new family of creation together–just as they would do with the more typical blood in-laws. It may also be a strategy that pushes lesbians to continue to prioritize their friendships, even as they engage in raising children of their own, maintaining and building connections with members of their families of origin, and/or pursuing new interests, including careers. Indeed, this pattern may fit well into the current historical era where, rather than there being one primary alliance–typically, in the era of lesbian feminism, to lesbian identity–it seems more accurate to say that lesbians recognize multiple alliances (Stein, 1997). Some lesbians at midlife today may create friends as family as one means by which they might sustain multiple alliances–to friends as well as to partner, children, family of origin members, and/or other individual interests including careers.

By including friends in their conceptions of families, even as they may build families with partners and children and seek to sustain ties with family of origin members, lesbians place themselves in a position to continue to challenge the definition of family, not only with respect to sex composition but also with respect to the emphasis on biological ties and "the relative weight given to friendships as well as blood relatedness" (Laird, 1993, p. 297; see also Nardi, 1992; Weston, 1991). With friends as a model for acceptance, respect, and appreciation–and as an option towards which they might turn for validation and support–lesbians may be more likely to demand similar treatment in their families of origin, leave such families when this treatment is not forthcoming, and create new families constructed upon these givens.

CONCLUSIONS

As more and more lesbians enter into and move through midlife during a historical time when lesbians are increasingly engaging in and gaining legitimacy for their partnership relationships and raising children, and fewer lesbians meet with automatic rejection from their families of origin, the time and energy available for friends may decrease and the necessity for friends to be as family may lessen. At the same time, the remembrance and continued presence of heterosexism in families of origin and the larger society, and the sense of familiarity, shared perspective, and shared experience among lesbian friends, may contribute to the continuing prioritization of lesbians' friendships among midlife lesbians. At this historical juncture, it appears that friends as family may be conceptualized by midlife lesbians in at least the three diverse ways described in this paper. It also appears that the first two of these patterns may be in decline; the extent to which the third pattern prevails depends upon a diversity of factors, some of which are addressed next.

Research. "Friends as family" has been a phrase often heard in the daily discourse of lesbians' lives and relied upon in the writings of researchers and theorists of lesbians' lives. Yet we know very little about the intended meaning of this phrase by those lesbians who use it. It is critical, then, that we attend more closely to individual lesbians' meanings of this phrase. As we study these meanings, however, it is critical that we begin to identify and study specific parameters that may influence the meanings of and possibilities for "friends as family." Current age, historical cohort, and age at time of coming out all warrant additional attention. We need as well to attend to the particular patterns of "friends as family" among lesbians in a couple relationship compared with those unintentionally or chosen single, whether they have or desire to have children, and whether and how they have sustained relationships with their families of origin. Most important, we need to take a longitudinal approach to the study of lesbians' friendships, as well as more consistently examine friendship patterns across a diversity of cohorts. It may be that the patterns of conceptualizing friends as family that I have described here are the result of movement through the adult developmental life course, and a corresponding movement towards acceptance and consolidation of a positive lesbian identity. On the other hand, it may be that historical changes and adult development patterns have coincided for the cohorts of lesbians in midlife today such that, for many, friends were initially experienced and constructed as substitute families in the early years of young adulthood and post-WW II. But this conception shifted to friends as a challenge to the family in the later years of young adulthood and the early years of the current feminist and lesbian liberation movements, and finally, it now reflects midlife lesbians' efforts, in the post-Stonewall, lesbian parenting boom era, to negotiate a place at the family table for friends, lovers, children, and families of origin.

In addition to examining cohort differences and developmental patterns over the course of adulthood, it is critical that we consider other aspects of lesbians' identities and experiences such as race, class, sex, religion, and ability. What are the experiences and conceptions of friends and families across a diversity of cultural communities, and how do these influence lesbians' experiences and conceptions of friends as family? The images of friendships painted in these pages reflect most closely the experiences and perspectives of white, middle-class lesbians.

Theory and practice. When working with midlife lesbians, it is critical that therapists and other social service providers consider friendships as a legitimate central component in lesbians' lives. But in order to hear and support lesbians who view friendships as central or equal to if not more important than current partner, children, and family of origin, it may be necessary for therapists and social workers to first consider and examine their own assumptions about the "proper" place of partner, friend, children, and family of origin. Not all midlife lesbians conceptualize, experience, or desire their friendships to be central, of course, and in some cases, such a structure may not work. Yet for those who have sought and been satisfied with such life structures, support has been limited in both theory and practice. Therapists and theorists alike must consider the desires of lesbians themselves, as well as the origins of developmental models that prioritize marriage and family for women. Rather than impose the prioritization of partner and family over friends, it is important to look at the particular situation and goals of the lesbians involved. In other words, theorists and social service providers may need to take care not to project mainstream–and their own–models of family and friendship onto midlife lesbians, but instead recognize the possibility of alternatives and listen to and help support the development of these alternative models of friends, family, and friends as family toward which some of the lesbians with whom they work or study may be striving.

The current challenge, I believe, is not to enforce or value any one pattern over another, but rather to preserve for lesbians the right and freedom to choose the pattern that best reflects their personal desires and best fits within their particular life choices and structures. Those who work with lesbians can do much to ensure that these options remain both equally available and respected. We may only do so, however, if we recognize that just as a central commitment to one's family of origin leaves less room for commitment to other forms of family and to friendship, those who are centrally committed to their friendships likely have less time and energy for parenting, partnering, and families of origin. Midlife lesbians may desire and negotiate a variety of ways of balancing among these relationship forms and commitments, in addition to their careers and community involvement. Practitioners need to take care not to privilege one manner of balancing these multiple possibilities over another.

Finally, I would caution therapists and theorists alike to keep their eyes on just what is being offered to lesbians in their families of origin as compared to their friendships, and to examine the costs and benefits of devoting energy to each. At the very least, lesbians' friendship families that provide a place where lesbians are accepted and respected as lesbians ought to serve as a guide to what is possible–and acceptable–in lesbians' families of origin (see also Brown, 1995). Indeed, lesbians' conceptions and experiences of friends as family may provide a powerful model for lesbians' relationships to their families of origin as well as procreation: to hold these families up to the ideal of friendship, striving to build family as friends, in addition to the other way around.

REFERENCES

Becker, C. S. (1988). *Unbroken ties: Lesbian ex-lovers.* Boston: Alyson Publications.

Bell, A. P., & Weinberg, M. S. (1978). *Homosexualities: A study of diversity among men and women.* New York: Simon & Schuster.

Blieszner, R., & Adams, R. G. (1992). *Adult friendship.* Newbury Park, CA: Sage.

Blumstein, P., & Schwartz, P. (1983). *American couples.* New York: William Morrow.

Bond, L. A., & Weinstock, J. S. (1997, March). The challenge of differing sexual identities to women's friendships. In J. S. Weinstock (Chair), *Lesbian friendship and social change.* Symposium conducted at the annual meetings of the Association for Women in Psychology, Pittsburgh, PA.

Bradford, J., & Ryan, C. (1988). *The National Lesbian Health Care Survey: Final report.* National Lesbian and Gay Health Foundation, Virginia Commonwealth University.

Bradford, J., & Ryan, C. (1991). Who we are: Health concerns of middle-aged lesbians. In B. Sang, J. Warshow, & A. J. Smith (Eds.), *Lesbians at midlife: The creative transition* (pp. 147-163). San Francisco: Spinsters Book Company.

Bradford, J., Ryan, C., & Rothblum, E. D. (1994). National Lesbian Health Care Survey: Implications for mental health care. *Journal of Consulting and Clinical Psychology, 62,* 228-242.

Brosnan, J. (1996). *Lesbians talk detonating the nuclear family.* London: Scarlett Press.

Brown, L. S. (1995). Are we family? Lesbians and families of origin. In K. Jay (Ed.), *Dyke life: From growing up to growing old, A celebration of the lesbian experience* (pp. 19-35). New York: Basic Books.

Bryant, S., & Demian (1994). Relationship characteristics of American gay and lesbian couples: Findings from a national survey. *Journal of Gay & Lesbian Social Services, 1,* 101-117.

Card, C. (1995). *Lesbian choices.* New York: Columbia University Press.

Clunis, D. M., & Green, G. D. (1988). *Lesbian couples: Creating healthy relationships for the '90s.* Seattle: Seal Press.

Daly, M. (Ed.). (1996). *Surface tension: Love, sex, and politics between lesbians and straight women.* New York: Simon & Schuster.

D'Augelli, A. R. (1989a). Lesbian women in a rural helping network: Exploring informal helping resources. *Women & Therapy, 8*(1/2), 119-130.

D'Augelli, A. R. (1989b). The development of a helping community for lesbians and gay men: A case study of community psychology. *Journal of Community Psychology, 17,* 18-29.

D'Augelli, A. R., Collins, C., & Hart, M. M. (1987). Social support patterns of lesbian women in a rural helping network. *Journal of Rural Community Psychology, 8*(1), 12-22.

D'Augelli, A. R., & Hart, M. M. (1987). Gay women, men, and families in rural settings: Toward the development of helping communities. *American Journal of Community Psychology, 15,* 79-93.

Demo, D. H., & Allen, K. R. (1996). Diversity within lesbian and gay families: Challenges and implications for family theory and research. *Journal of Social and Personal Relationships, 13,* 415-434.

Diamond, L. M. (1997, March). *Passionate friendships: Love and attachment among young lesbian, bisexual, and heterosexual women.* Invited paper presented to the annual meetings of the Association for Women in Psychology, Pittsburgh, PA.

Faderman, L. (1991). *Odd girls and twilight lovers: A history of lesbian life in twentieth-century America.* New York: Columbia University Press.

Friend, R. A. (1989). Older lesbian and gay people: Responding to homophobia. *Marriage & Family Review, 14,* 241-263.

Futcher, J., & Hopkins, C. (1996). Heart like a wheel: A friendship in two voices. In J. S. Weinstock & E. D. Rothblum (Eds.), *Lesbian friendships: For ourselves and each other* (pp. 65-79). New York: New York University Press.

Gergen, M. M. (1990). Finished at 40: Women's development within the patriarchy. *Psychology of Women Quarterly, 14,* 471-493.

Grammick, J. (1984). Developing a lesbian identity. In T. Darty & S. Potter (Eds.), *Women identified women* (pp. 31-44). Palo Alto, CA: Mayfield.

Grana, S. J. (1989). *The friendship triangle: The relationship between expectations, experiences and satisfaction for dyadic and nondyadic heterosexual women and lesbians.* Unpublished doctoral dissertation, University of Nebraska, Lincoln, NE.

Hall, R., & Rose, S. (1996). Friendships between African-American and white lesbians. In J. S. Weinstock & E. D. Rothblum (Eds.), *Lesbians friendships: For ourselves and each other* (pp. 165-191). New York: New York University Press.

Hetrick, E. S., & Martin, A. D. (1987). Developmental issues and their resolution for gay and lesbian adolescents. *Journal of Homosexuality, 14,* 25-43.

Hite, S. (1987). *Women in love: A cultural revolution in progress.* New York: Alfred A. Knopf.

Hoagland, S. L. (1988). *Lesbian ethics: Toward new value.* Palo Alto, CA: Institute of Lesbian Studies.

Hoagland, S. L. (1992). Introduction. In J. Penelope, *Call me lesbian: Lesbian lives, lesbian theory* (pp. xi-xvii). Freedom, CA: The Crossing Press.

Jo, B. (1996). Lesbian friendships create lesbian community. In J. S. Weinstock & E. D. Rothblum (Eds.), *Lesbian friendships: For ourselves and each other* (pp. 288-291). New York: New York University Press.

Kennedy, L. L., & Davis, M. (1993). *Boots of leather, slippers of gold: The history of a lesbian community.* New York: Routledge.

Kimmel, D. C. (1992). The families of older gay men and lesbians. *Generations, 17*(3), 37-38.

Kimmel, D. C., & Sang, B. E. (1995). Lesbians and gay men in midlife. In A. R. D'Augelli & C. J. Patterson (Eds.), *Lesbian, gay, and bisexual identities over the lifespan: Psychological perspectives* (pp. 190-214). New York: Oxford University Press.

Kirkpatrick, M. (1989). Lesbians: A different middle-age? In J. Oldham & R. Liebert (Eds.), *New psychoanalytic perspectives: The middle years* (pp. 135-148). New Haven, CT: Yale University Press.

Kitzinger, C. (1996). Toward a politics of lesbian friendship. In J. S. Weinstock & E. D. Rothblum (Eds.), *Lesbian friendships: For ourselves and each other* (pp. 295-299). New York: New York University Press.

Kitzinger, C., and Perkins, R. (1993). *Changing our minds: Lesbian feminism and psychology.* New York: New York University Press.

Kurdek, L. A. (1988). Perceived social support in gays and lesbians in cohabiting relationships. *Journal of Personality and Social Psychology, 54,* 504-509.

Kurdek, L. A. (1995). Developmental changes in relationship quality in gay and lesbian cohabiting couples. *Developmental Psychology, 31,* 86-94.

Kurdek, L. A., & Schmitt, J. P. (1987). Perceived support from family and friends in members of homosexual, married, and heterosexual cohabiting couples. *Journal of Homosexuality, 14,* 57-68.

Kus, R. J. (1991). Sobriety, friends, and gay men. *Archives of Psychiatric Nursing, 5,* 171-177.

Laird, J. (1993). Gay and lesbian families. In F. Walsh (Ed.), *Normal family processes,* 2nd ed. (pp. 282-328). New York: The Guilford Press.

Levinson, D. J. (1978). *The seasons of a man's life.* New York: Ballantine Books.

Levinson, D. J. (1996). *The seasons of a woman's life.* New York: Alfred A. Knopf.

Lewin, E. (1993). *Lesbian mothers: Accounts of gender in American culture.* Ithaca, NY: Cornell University Press.

Lewin, E. (1996). "Why in the world would you want to do that?" Claiming community in lesbian commitment. In E. Lewin (Ed.), *Inventing lesbian culture in America* (pp. 105-130). Boston: Beacon Press.

Lipman, A. (1986). Homosexual relationships. *Generations: Quarterly Journal of the American Society on Aging, 10*(4), 51-54.

Loulan, J. (1991). "Now when I was your age": One perspective on how lesbian culture has influenced sexuality. In B. Sang, J. Warshow, & A. J. Smith (Eds.), *Lesbians at midlife: The creative transition* (pp. 10-18). San Francisco: Spinsters Book Company.

MacLean, J. (1995). An afternoon with my if-there-were-a-laws. In K. Jay (Ed.), *Dyke life: From growing up to growing old, A celebration of the lesbian experience* (p. 23). New York: Basic Books.

Munson, M. (1996). Celebrating wild erotic friendship: Marcia and Martha. In J. S. Weinstock & E. D. Rothblum (Eds.), *Lesbian friendships: For ourselves and each other* (pp. 125-132). New York: New York University Press.

Nardi, P. M. (1982). Alcohol treatment and the non-traditional "family" structures of gays and lesbians. *Journal of Alcohol and Drug Education, 27*(2), 83-89.

Nardi, P. M. (1992). That's what friends are for: Friends as family in the gay and lesbian community. In K. Plummer (Ed.), *Modern homosexualities: Fragments of lesbian and gay experience* (pp. 108-120). New York: Routledge.

Nardi, P. M., & Sherrod, D. (1994). Friendships in the lives of gay men and lesbians. *Journal of Social and Personal Relationships, 11,* 185-199.

O'Boyle, C. G., & Thomas, M. D. (1996). Friendships between lesbian and heterosexual women. In J. S. Weinstock & E. D. Rothblum (Eds.), *Lesbian friendships: For ourselves and each other* (pp. 240-248). New York: New York University Press.

O'Connor, P. (1992). *Friendships between women: A critical review.* New York: The Guilford Press.

Palladino, D., & Stephenson, Y. (1990). Perceptions of the sexual self: Their impact on relationships between lesbian and heterosexual women. *Women & Therapy, 9,* 231-253.

Patterson, C. J. (1992). Children of lesbian and gay parents. *Child Development, 63,* 1025-1042.

Patterson, C. J. (1995a). Families of the lesbian baby boom: Parents' division of labor and children's adjustment. *Developmental Psychology, 31,* 115-123.

Patterson, C. J. (1995b). Lesbian mothers, gay fathers, and their children. In A. R. D'Augelli & C. J. Patterson (Eds.), *Lesbian, gay, and bisexual identities over the lifespan: Psychological perspectives* (pp. 262-290). New York: Oxford University Press.

Patterson, C. J. (1996). Contributions of lesbian and gay parents and their children to the prevention of heterosexism. In E. D. Rothblum & L. A. Bond (Eds.), *Preventing heterosexism and homophobia* (pp. 184-201). Thousand Oaks, CA: Sage.

Patterson, C. J., & Redding, R. E. (1996). Lesbian and gay families with children: Implications of social service research for policy. *Journal of Social Issues, 52,* 29-50.

Peplau, L. A. (1993). Lesbian and gay relationships. In L D. Garnets & D. C. Kimmel (Eds.), *Psychological perspectives on lesbian and gay male experiences* (pp. 395-419). New York: Columbia University Press.

Pred, E. (1996). Healing group. In M. Adelman (Ed.), *Lesbian passages: True stories told by women over 40* (pp. 51-57). Los Angeles: Alyson Publications. (Originally published 1986.)

Raphael, S., & Robinson, M. (1984). The older lesbian: Love relationships and friendship patterns. In T. Darty & S. Potter (Eds.), *Women-identified women* (pp. 67-82). Palo Alto, CA: Mayfield.

Raymond, J. G. (1986). *A passion for friends: Towards a philosophy of female affection.* Boston: Beacon Press.

Raymond, J. G. (1990). Not a sentimental journey: Women's friendships. In D. Leidholdt & J. G. Raymond (Eds.), *The sexual liberals and the attack on feminism.* London: Pergamon.

Reid, J. D. (1995). Development in late life: Older lesbian and gay lives. In A. R. D'Augelli & C. J. Patterson (Eds.), *Lesbian, gay, and bisexual identities over the lifespan: Psychological perspectives* (pp. 215-240). New York: Oxford University Press.

Rose, S. (1996). Lesbian and gay love scripts. In E. D. Rothblum & L. A. Bond (Eds.), *Preventing heterosexism and homophobia* (pp. 151-173). Thousand Oaks, CA: Sage.

Rose, S., Zand, D., & Cini, M A. (1993). Lesbian courtship scripts. In E. D. Rothblum & K. A. Brehony (Eds.), *Boston marriages: Romantic but asexual relationships among contemporary lesbians* (pp. 70-85). Amherst: The University of Massachusetts Press.

Rothblum, E. D. (1994). Transforming lesbian sexuality. *Psychology of Women Quarterly, 18,* 627-641.

Rothblum, E. D., & Brehony, K. A. (1993). *Boston marriages: Romantic but asexual relationships among contemporary lesbians.* Amherst: The University of Massachusetts Press.

Rothblum, E. D., Mintz, B., Cowan, D. B., & Haller, C. (1995). Lesbian baby boomers at midlife. In K. Jay (Ed.), *Dyke life: From growing up to growing old, A celebration of the lesbian experience* (pp. 61-76). New York: Basic Books.

Rust, P. C. (1995). *The challenge of bisexuality to lesbian politics: Sex, loyalty, and revolution.* New York: New York University Press.

Saghir, M. T., & Robins, E. (1973). *Male and female homosexuality: A comprehensive investigation.* Baltimore: Williams & Wilkins.

Sang, B. (1991). Moving towards balance and integration. In B. Sang, J. Warshow, & A. Smith (Eds.), *Lesbians at midlife: The creative transition* (pp. 206-214). San Francisco: Spinsters Ink.

Savin-Williams, R. C. (1995). Lesbian, gay male, and bisexual adolescents. In A. R. D'Augelli & C. J. Patterson (Eds.), *Lesbian, gay, and bisexual identities over the lifespan: Psychological perspectives* (pp. 165-189). New York: Oxford University Press.

Shernoff, M. J. (1984). Family therapy for lesbian and gay clients. *Social Work, 29,* 393-396.

Slater, S. (1994). Approaching and avoiding the work of the middle years: Affairs in committed lesbian relationships. *Women & Therapy, 15*(2), 19-34.

Slater, S. (1995). *The lesbian family life cycle.* New York: The Free Press.

Slater, S., & Mencher, J. (1991). The lesbian family life cycle: A contextual approach. *American Journal of Orthopsychiatry, 61,* 372-382.

Smolak, L. (1993). *Adult development.* Englewood Cliffs, NJ: Prentice-Hall.

Stanley, J. L. (1996). The lesbian's experience of friendship. In J. S. Weinstock & E. D. Rothblum (Eds.), *Lesbian friendships: For ourselves and each other* (pp. 39-59). New York: New York University Press.

Stein, A. (1997). *Sex and sensibility: Stories of a lesbian generation.* Berkeley, CA: University of California Press.

Stewart, A. J., & Gold-Steinberg, S. (1990). Midlife women's political consciousness. *Psychology of Women Quarterly, 14,* 543-566.

Strega, L. (1996). A lesbian love story. In J. S. Weinstock & E. D. Rothblum (Eds.), *Lesbian friendships: For ourselves and each other* (pp. 277-287). New York: New York University Press.

Tully, C. (1989). Caregiving: What do midlife lesbians view as important? *Journal of Gay & Lesbian Psychotherapy, 1,* 87-103.

Vetere, V. A. (1982). The role of friendship in the development and maintenance of lesbian love relationships. *Journal of Homosexuality, 8*(2), 51-65.

Weinstock, J. S. (in press). Examining the forms, functions, and meanings of friendships for adult lesbians, gay men, bisexual women and men, and transgender persons. Chapter to be published in A. R. D'Augelli & C. J. Patterson (Eds.), *Lesbian, gay, and bisexual families.*

Weinstock, J. S., & Rothblum, E. D. (Eds.). (1996a). *Lesbian friendships: For ourselves and each other.* New York: New York University Press.

Weinstock, J. S., & Rothblum, E. D. (1996b). What we can be together: Contemplating lesbians' friendships. In J. S. Weinstock & E. D. Rothblum (Eds.), *Lesbian friendships: For ourselves and each other* (pp. 3-30). New York: New York University Press.

Weston, K. (1991). *Families we choose: Lesbians, gays, kinship.* New York: Columbia University Press.

Weston, K. (1996). Requiem for a street fighter. In E. Lewin (Ed.), *Inventing lesbian culture in America* (pp. 131-141). Boston: Beacon Press.

The Bloom Is on the Rose:
The Impact of Midlife
on the Lesbian Couple

Valory Mitchell

SUMMARY. This paper argues for the value of an adult developmental perspective in work with lesbian couples. Focusing on midlife, case examples illustrate issues and situations that create strength and satisfaction, as well as those that create stress and disappointment. Key themes include expansiveness and generativity, differentiation, awareness of past and future, reorganizing priorities, finitude, caregiving stress, infidelity, midlife crisis, self-growth, and the different impact of homophobia on three cohorts of midlife lesbians. Implications for therapeutic intervention are described, with particular emphasis on case formulation and treatment planning that explicitly provides couples with an understanding of the sociohistorical and adult developmental context in which their difficulties arise. *[Article copies available for a fee from The Haworth Document Delivery Service: 1-800-342-9678. E-mail address: <getinfo@haworthpressinc.com> Website: <http://www.haworthpressinc.com>]*

KEYWORDS. Midlife, lesbian, couples, parenting, infidelity, caregivers, women, family, adult development, homophobia

"THE" MIDLIFE LESBIAN COUPLE (?)

There are many kinds of midlife lesbian couples. Each is unique in the uniqueness of the personal qualities, talents, and history of the two

---

Valory Mitchell, PhD, is Associate Professor at the California School of Professional Psychology, Alameda, CA, and a Psychotherapist in private practice.

[Haworth co-indexing entry note]: "The Bloom Is on the Rose: The Impact of Midlife on the Lesbian Couple." Mitchell, Valory. Co-published simultaneously in *Journal of Gay & Lesbian Social Services* (Harrington Park Press, an imprint of The Haworth Press, Inc.) Vol. 11, No. 2/3, 2000, pp. 33-48; and: *Midlife Lesbian Relationships: Friends, Lovers, Children, and Parents* (ed: Marcy R. Adelman) Harrington Park Press, an imprint of The Haworth Press, Inc., 2000, pp. 33-48. Single or multiple copies of this article are available for a fee from The Haworth Document Delivery Service [1-800-342-9678, 9:00 a.m. - 5:00 p.m. (EST). E-mail address: getinfo@haworthpressinc.com].

33

individuals who come together, and the particular combinations of allegiances that shape the identity of each partner–class, ethnicity, geography, culture. A midlife lesbian couple may be thriving, filled with vitality; or burdened and depleted by the stresses of life's demands and the inevitable disappointments of a less-than-perfect partner (as well as one's less-than-perfect self!). The couple may be foundering, frightened, and lost as unexpected developmental pressures, new situations, and unresolved discontents erupt. Or they may have weathered those storms, so that now the two stalwart survivors repair the damage, rebuild, and renew. In addition, midlife lesbian couples occupy every point on the continuum of the lesbian family cycle (Slater, 1995): Midlife couples include new couples who have just met and fallen in love, couples who have been together long enough to want to "put down roots," as well as couples who have woven the fabric of a shared life structure–a home, a family, a history, a future.

What all these very different couples have in common is the presence of one, or two, women who find themselves at that "certain age"–no longer young, but not yet old–that constitutes midlife.

This paper will consider whether that makes any difference–and, if it does, what difference it may make. When midlife imperatives create a painful and destructive context for the lesbian couple, we must also ask what difference *we* can make as mental health professionals. In this paper, I will draw from my experience with patients and consultees, and from interviews with individuals and couples who agreed to talk with me about their views of midlife. I am grateful to each of you for this contribution, and for your candor and courage.

The Best of Times, the Worst of Times . . .

At best. The quarter century that spans midlife, 40-65, is for many women a time of expansion (Stewart & Gold-Steinberg, 1990). Most women in midlife have built an adult life structure–one that holds a scnse of accomplishment and achievement; that contains one's history and prior goals; that continues to ask major commitments of time, energy, and resources of all kinds; that continues to ground them in a daily experience that feels purposive and worthwhile. Life's lessons have brought perspective, confidence, and competence. Midlife brings many women the time, energy, and resources to add new "experiential worlds" (Hornstein, 1986) of paid or volunteer work; artistic, spiritual, or political activity; family and friendships; or leisure endeavors to their life structure.

Kindled by a deepening awareness of the inevitability of one's own personal ending (Gould, 1978; Jaques, 1965), midlife also brings a reorganizing of priorities. For some, these shifts reflect an expanded concern with generativity–creating and offering a legacy or contribution that expresses the wish to give something back that will last longer than one's self and will provide something of value to those who come after (Erikson, 1950). Strengths and capacities that are ascendant at midlife (Neugarten, 1968) are often mobilized in this effort to reach out (Stewart & Gold-Steinberg, op. cit.).

When lesbian couples unite in generativity, both the couple and the community are enriched. Del Martin and Phyllis Lyon, the couple who founded America's first lesbian organization, Daughters of Bilitis, produced some of their most noteworthy achievements during midlife–authoring together *Lesbian/Woman,* one of the first realistic books about the lesbian experience (Martin & Lyon, 1972/1991).

For most women, midlife change emerges within a context of stability and represents planful expression and extension, based on a continuity of values. These are the women (and couples) who sail through midlife with relative equanimity (Wrightsman, 1988) or even ascendance (Neugarten, 1968). Studies of heterosexual women's life span development (Mitchell & Helson, 1990) indicate that, for women generally, midlife may be the "prime of life"–a first-rate time of vigor and satisfaction, when life is moving well. Although data are unavailable, it seems likely that these findings generalize to lesbian women.

Cindy and Cherise: It really works. One of the most usual ways to manifest generativity is by raising children, who carry forward (one hopes) energy and ideals that link the personal past with the future. In this example, the strength of two women, committed to each other and to shared values, allows them to further their generative priorities in ways that neither could accomplish alone.

Cindy and Cherise agreed to tell me about ways their lives are different now, as a lesbian couple in which both partners are in midlife. At their request, we met after work, over dinner at a casual Italian restaurant in their neighborhood. Cherise spoke first. They go back a long way together, now, and their common ethnic heritage (both are from Italian-American families) gives them a feeling of common ground that goes back even further. Midlife? Well, Cherise went on, earlier in their relationship, she had thought that if she just presented her point of view clearly enough and often enough, it would change Cindy's mind. As the years have passed, she has come to accept that Cindy is . . . well . . . Cindy. (And, Cindy interjected, Cherise is certainly still Cherise!)

Theorists and therapists who study and work with couples recognize here the hard-won differentiation that enables couples to move beyond the "honeymoon" of what they share, and to enjoy the clarity with which they can recognize (usually lovingly) the separate and different self of the partner.

In their years together, they have listened and encouraged each other as professional careers were built, debts were paid, and incomes grew. They wanted children, and held each other through the vulnerability and disappointments of fertility problems, miscarriages, and the uncertainties of the adoption process. Now, their two school-aged children bring them delight, challenge, tenderness, burdens, an erosion of their time for and with each other, an enlargement of their lives.

Wanting to increase the children's time with a parent each day, Cindy has decided to work part-time. This midlife change alters the configuration of their days, and of their relationship. Yes, she says, her large eyes widening, looked at in one way, it seems like a good move, a sensible move, the best move, and a move taken at the right time. But, looked at in another way, Cindy smiles ruefully, the whole picture changes, and she sees a midlife woman in a part-time job, at home with the kids, financially dependent on a partner, a "sitting duck" whom any feminist worth her salt would comfort and then counsel. What an attractive picture . . . she glances at Cherise.

Suddenly, Cherise is in motion. She pulls a thick felt pen from her pocket and goes to work, scribbling furiously in large letters on the butcher paper that substitutes for a tablecloth. Finished, she rips the newly created document from the larger sheet and hands it over: "I AM COMMITTED TO SUPPORT CINDY SHOULD WE SPLIT. BUT WE WON'T. (SIGNED) C. LA COPA."

> Cindy bursts into laughter, also wipes a tear, and hands the paper to me. Here, she says, this is what midlife is about for lesbian couples.

Clinical implications. In that moment, I felt the past, present, and future seated with us as tangibly as additional diners. These guests accompany midlife women–whether individually, in couples, or in larger gatherings–through the sudden glimmer of a shared memory, the hint of fear about an always uncertain old age. When, as with Cindy and Cherise, they are welcomed to the table, they bring a depth and richness to the experience and possibilities of midlife.

I believe that this couple would respond in the same way, regardless of the focus of change. Instead of time for children, perhaps it would have been time for artistic or humanitarian action, a career change, or geographic upheaval. As a thriving midlife couple, they can address shared or individual goals that cry out for attention and nurturance with the same openness, consideration, and sturdy flexibility and commitment.

While couples like Cindy and Cherise are unlikely to seek therapy, it may be useful for mental health professionals to hold in mind the everyday strengths that they embody. First, this couple has a comfortable clarity about collaboration and differentiation. Together, they have created a way of life that neither could individually have made, yet they are not merged in any detrimental or pathological way. Quite the contrary, this couple manifests an intersubjectivity and mutuality that contemporary relational theorists (Jordan, 1986; Miller, 1986) have offered as evidence of psychological maturity and vitality. Second, they do not take on one another's insecurities, do not feel accused, and so do not need to be defensive. This allows them to come forward in ways that convey acceptance, support, and comfort. Whether it be Cindy's lighthearted reminder that Cherise is a vivid and visible presence, or Cherise's declaration to counter Cindy's (age-linked) fears of abandonment, each was able to address the other's worry without feeling blamed–a tragically common roadblock for couples whose trust and appreciation of each other has eroded or been damaged. Finally, just as they are accepting and open to each other, they accept the legacy that their pasts have brought and remain open to the opportunities, the sorrows, and the ambiguity that their future holds. This long view in both directions is a hallmark of midlife; it can also be an invaluable asset of effectively functioning couples.

WHEN LESBIAN COUPLES SEEK HELP

I have said that midlife may be the best of times, the worst of times. In our work, we more often encounter women whose journey through midlife is difficult and depleting, or even profoundly troubling and dangerous. We must be careful not to overgeneralize; most lesbian couples find great pleasure and security in the comfort and expansiveness of midlife. At the same time, many couples experience layers of chronic stress that makes theirs a life characterized more by endurance than by satisfaction. And, for others, midlife feels like a tornado–a whirlwind of uncontrollable forces that touch down at random, covering the sky with dust and debris and, sometimes, threatening to tear everything apart.

Endurance: The Dual-Career, Dual-Caregiver Family

Because lesbian couples are formed by two women–and because women are on the "front lines" in caring both for the elderly and infirm as well as for the young and growing (Carstensen & Pasupathi, 1993)–these couples can find themselves "sandwiched" between the needs of elders and youth as well as the demands of the workplace, with scant remaining time or energy for themselves as individuals or as a couple.

Are we only a bridge? Willow and Nelda. They weren't in trouble . . . yet. That is how Nelda, the more outgoing partner, began our first session of couples therapy. But they bicker so often now, finding fault or going on the defensive. Their lives are very full and busy, but it used to be that they experienced their time together as replenishing, intimate, where each felt the most visible and the most appreciated. Willow listens, her lips forming a thin, tense line. When Nelda finished, Willow sighed. How long can we keep on like this?

As we looked together at the shape of their days, it became apparent that, out of love, they had asked themselves to place the needs of others first for so long. So that a parent could be home with daughter Susan after school, Willow arrived at work at 6:00 a.m. Consequently, there was almost no private time for the couple after their daughter went to bed. Then, too, Nelda often stopped at her mother's home after work. After months of the flu, the older woman was weak and needed extra help, as well as company.

We live in a culture and time in history that require most couples to be dual earners. Many of us skate narrowly close to the kind of depletion that can shorten our patience and lengthen our discontent. Under conditions of chronic depletion, some part of the self rises in anger and frustration–as it should. But, if these feelings become displaced toward one's "nearest and dearest," it can feel as if one's partner is unsupportive, when actually it is our way of life that is demanding too much. A cycle of misunderstanding begins, accusations are met with defense, and neither partner feels able to create change.

Clinical implications. A first step is to return the blame to where it belongs. Therapists and other mental health professionals can provide both partners with much-needed soothing and comforting simply by offering a clear recognition and acknowledgement of the enormity, immediacy, and importance of the tasks undertaken, as well as the ongoing effort and good intent of each partner. As the "blame" for chronic stress is located in the situation, each can again recognize and appreciate her partner's hard work, caring actions, and sacrifices. And she, in turn, can feel seen and valued by her partner. They each re-kindle their alliance, united as they rise to the challenges that life has brought.

A second intervention that may require the therapist as advocate is permission and initiative-taking to create regular "doses" of duty-free time for the couple to be alone together. Willow and Nelda decided to experiment with lunch together twice a week. Although fearful that they would be unable to meet without bringing out their "lists of undone tasks," they found that they could carve out a work-free inter-lude to simply experience the pleasure of each other's company. While each was hungry for this experience, they had "painted themselves into a corner" where, when one suggested it, the other would use the request as an opportunity to express that *she* (presumably unlike the partner) had to meet life's demands and couldn't just "hang out." It took the therapist, who stood outside this dynamic, to persevere in advocating both the moral legitimacy and the logistical possibility of creating these interludes.

That summer, Willow and Nelda took a week at a (lesbian-owned alternative-family) family camp. As Susan enjoyed her time with other young campers, her mothers hiked, talked . . . even, for the first time in a very long time, made love.

As the therapy progressed and they understood the sociohistorical and adult developmental context of their problems, Willow and Nelda were increasingly able to appreciate each other and feel appreciated in turn. We were able to engage work on communications and issues of transference that make up the regular repertoire of individual and couples therapy treatments.

A final midlife intervention was particularly valuable to them: We began to consider the future. This was a poignant aspect of our work, because the stresses of caring for an aging parent and a young child are relieved when the parent dies and the child grows up. As they were able to take perspective on their midlife situation, they came to recognize both the richness of the precious, fleeting moments of time with young children and with aging parents, and also the relentless stress of having more demands than there is time to meet them. For Willow and Nelda, imagining an easier future together was itself healing.

The Worst of Times: "Extramarital" Affairs in Midlife

For yet other couples, the term "midlife crisis" is neither a joke nor an exaggeration (Whitbourne, 1986). Caught in psychological or interpersonal storms that are so intense, these women can only "tie themselves to the mast" and hope they will not be thrown overboard as their "ship" is tossed about in a sea of tumult. For them, the same developmental themes that bring some women added energy to place in constructive action and fulfillment have a darker aspect.

A couple's adult life structure is shaped not only by their combined skills, goals, and values, but also by what was not chosen, what each partner has been afraid of or unable to do, and what has been sacrificed (perhaps for good reasons, but sacrificed nonetheless). In midlife, one recognizes (though perhaps not consciously) that what is missing now may always be missing, as the future ceases to be felt as without end (Jaques, 1965). The illnesses or deaths of friends, relatives, and public figures underscore this. Jung (1960) notes that it is particularly at this time of life when neglected or underdeveloped aspects of the self press for recognition and nurturance.

A moth to a flame. When these parts of the self come knocking, demanding attention, they may feel threatening or disruptive. Perhaps because of this, they often come in disguise. For the lesbian couple, this occurs most traumatically when one partner locates these neglected or underdeveloped aspects of herself in another person. Then, it feels as if that person enlivens and completes the self in a way that is compelling. The relationship with such a person is easily eroticized and includes the powerful component of urgency.

The experience of an enhanced self that seems to be brought about through the presence, encouragement, and delight reflected in the eyes of the lover catapults the midlife woman and her partner into an electric, chaotic, wrenching situation.

Lena's story. Lena, age 53, sits on the edge of the big, old, stuffed chair in my office. She angles her head down, seeming to focus on the rug in front of her. As she does, her long hair falls forward. She unclenches her hands, moves one up to push the hair–honey colored, with strands of silver–back from her face. She has come because her partner, Carrie (and Carrie's therapist) think it might help "to see someone."

Carrie, Lena tells me, is a wonderful woman–intelligent, articulate, attractive, thoughtful. They have been together 13 years, and she has "never felt so loved as with Carrie." Together, they have enjoyed successful careers and a circle of good friends, sharing music and films, traveling occasionally, gardening in the yard of the home they own. But Lena has not spent one night in their home in the past four months. Instead, she is staying in a friend's spare bedroom . . . and seeing Meredith.

For the last couple of years, and by her own design, Lena's life had been dominated by work and school. Wanting to enter more purposive and challenging work, she had taken on a weekend college program that was difficult–and school had never been her home.

It had been springtime, the season for which Lena (who loves to be outdoors and on the move) had been waiting. Springtime was also when Meredith was transferred to Lena's workplace. Lena discovered Meredith's "shoot-from-the-hip" spontaneity, her quick sense of humor; she began to lighten up. She enjoyed her time at work with Meredith, then their lunch hours together. She found herself wanting to introduce Meredith, who was new to the region, to the natural beauty of the area. The energy between them built.

Carrie had been Lena's partner for 13 years. She knew Lena well and could not miss the difference in Lena's voice as she spoke with Meredith on the phone. The painful dialogue between them began, as Carrie and Lena decided together that Lena needed to explore, and it would be less painful if Carrie did not have to know the details of her coming and going.

By the time I met her, Lena was no longer entirely enveloped in the rushing energy of her affair with Meredith. Tearful and torn, she had awakened to a situation in which there could only be loss. And she felt she could not bear any of the possible losses.

Repetition and mastery of old conflicts. A midlife affair often symbolizes a repetition of the relationship constellations of early years. As a child, Lena had felt torn between her parents. Mother and grandmother were steady, and present, but serious and bound by religion and sexism to narrow and diligent lives. Times with father were vacation times, more fun. Days with his family were feast days, loud, bustling, and energized–special days.

As she made her life choices, Lena had drifted unconsciously, more and more over the years, toward a diligent and serious way. Carrie accommodated to it, out of love for Lena and respect for her choices; Carrie's slower tempo and more reflective personal style were compatible with the consistency of their days. But their time together was rarely playful and spontaneous. With her attraction to Meredith, Lena had returned to the configuration of her childhood: a secure but somewhat depressed home life, and suddenly the chance for a "vacation" with the fun-loving energy of someone new.

A pull toward integration. Lena came to therapy recognizing that she could not bear to lose either her life with Carrie or the experience she was having with Meredith. Put into other terms, she needed to have a self that was both secure and steady, as well as playful and spontaneous. Only with the harmonious union of the two aspects of herself could she regain her sense of vitality.

When this conflict is enacted in the "outer" world, actual people are recruited to bring out aspects of the self. The transformations are unexpected, hard to explain. For example, someone who has always thought of herself as sexually inhibited, or without purpose, will be entirely different with the lover. It becomes her midlife work (with or without therapy) to recognize that these are neglected aspects of the self that do not reside only in the lover. Lena began to acknowledge that, despite the fears and worries that had characterized her young adulthood, she was a person who had a spirit of adventure and longed to be lighthearted. Could she be, without Meredith to cause it?

Could she be? This question forms the pivot on which midlife development builds. What will be the self, and the life, which take shape? What modifications must occur so that, in the last phase of life, we can have the integrity to embrace the one and only life that we have had?

The baby and the bath water. Lena would say, "I'm on vacation from my life." And that is how she saw it. Although she felt she could not bear a life "in the gray zone," lacking the lightheartedness she had known with Meredith, she did not want to leave Carrie–Carrie was central to her life.

And Carrie was choosing to wait, to stay accessible. She told Lena that almost everyone with whom she had spoken had said they would never allow a partner to "do this to me." But Carrie seemed to recognize that this was not about her. At times, she became angry and sad that her pain alone could not alter Lena from her path. Yet she had chosen Lena, built a life with her, and wanted her back. And the fabric of their shared history and hopes, respect and intimacy, might form a safety net to protect them as their life together seemed to plummet toward destruction.

In my experience, and contrary to what seems to be popular belief, many women in long-term lesbian relationships choose to endure the firestorm of their partner's affair and go on to grieve together and rebuild. And many affairs extinguish, seeming almost to burn out by themselves.

Lena's struggle may lead to the dismantling of the couple relationship; perhaps evolving to a friendship, perhaps not. On the other hand, it may bring her newly into that relationship as a midlife woman with energy, greater capacity, and a stronger and more consolidated sense of self. If so, Carrie and Lena will not go back to live as they had before–nor would they wish to do so. Instead, they may "rise from the ashes," embodying a theme of decline and rebirth that vividly represents the symbolism of midlife.

Clinical implications. For the therapist, staying to bear witness to the ricocheting emotions and impulses of the midlife affair is a demanding task. The ongoing shifts and instability of the client's perspective and circumstances create a precarious environment for empathy and fertile ground for the therapist's countertransference. The therapist may become tempted to create order where it is not, by choosing sides, by deciding that one or another person in the triangle should depart, or shape up, or be left, or leave. However, if we take an adult developmental perspective and recognize that all participants are also actors in a projected drama of intrapsychic struggles for growth and integration, then it would be a profoundly antitherapeutic collusion with the client's fears of growth to try to dismiss anyone (or any facet of the self) from her place at the table.

Instead, it becomes the therapist's task to interpret the action of this drama in psychological terms, so that the client can recognize and begin to grapple with the internal issues of self-growth that have been symbolized by the dilemma. Because core conflicts are engaged and the stakes are so high on all sides, clients often experience great relief when the therapist is able to see (and describe) the larger picture.

THREADS OF THE MIDLIFE DEVELOPMENTAL FABRIC

Lena's experience illustrates several themes that unite the midlife affair with other changes that are common to midlife psychological development. The sense of urgency is not unlike that uncanny sense of finitude that "lights a fire" under the nonromantic projects of midlife lesbians (and other people as well). The need to expand the self is a midlife theme–and a theme that is much more prominent in midlife affairs than in the triangulations that can occur at other ages.

Standing on the pinnacle of midlife, one can look very far–both back into the past and ahead into the future. This "view from the summit" can be enacted in relation to aging parents and growing children, or with the elders and youth that make up our "communities of choice." The repetition and re-working of old conflicts, and their mastery and integration to make a more expansive self and life for the future, is enacted in the midlife affair, just as it is (more benignly for the couple) in the joint authorship of a book, the raising of one's children, and activism on behalf of long-cherished human values.

Midlife Psychological Themes Unique to Lesbians

If midlife is bounded by ages 40-65, then midlife today includes all those lesbians born between 1935 and 1960. The oldest were children during World War II, and teen-agers in the 1950s–an era of cozy conservatism that sent women out of the paid workforce and into a dream of suburban heterosexist domesticity. They grew up on radio, not television. There was no concept of gay rights, no gay organization, no women's movement for these young lesbian women. One's lesbian identity, life choices, and couple choices were forged in a context of isolation and stigma that is difficult for younger women to fathom.

The second cohort of lesbian midlifers is part of the demographic bulge known as the post-war baby boom. They were children in the 1950s, watching "Father Knows Best" on television, reading "Dick and Jane." In their teen years, the civil rights movement overlapped with anti-war activism. If they looked hard, at age 20, they could find one "lesbian homophile organization" that fielded phone calls from throughout the nation. The grassroots consciousness-raising of the early women's movement, the hippies, Stonewall, and the first notion of gay rights painted a backdrop for the lesbian identity they forged in their early adult years, and for the couple relationships they have had.

A third cohort, those in their early 40s, cannot remember the 1950s, or life before television or rock-and-roll. Too young for peace marches and the counterculture, they entered a very different adult world. Many of these lesbian couples expect to have commitment ceremonies to celebrate with family and friends; expect to become two-mom families, with children conceived through alternative insemination; expect to come together with thousands of lesbians, dancing and dining together in the grand ballrooms of nationally known luxury hotels.

The women of these three historical cohorts have created very different lesbian lives and have made their choices, and understood the meaning of their choices, very differently. In part, these differences exist because, as they forged their identities in the era of their early adult years, they did so in such different socio-historical contexts.

Many midlife lesbians follow closely the changes in the climate of the women's community. They recognize the greater ease, the vastly greater smorgasbord of opportunities that characterizes the life space of younger cohorts of lesbians. This relative loosening of oppression, brought in part through the midwifery of the older midlife lesbians, is a source of considerable pride. However, as the more universal midlife themes intersect, some lesbians may want to modify their lives in ways that seem almost to "jump" across cohorts, to attempt to leave behind the pervasive cultural shaming which has constrained their experience across the years (Schoonmaker, 1993).

Sowing the seeds of the final challenge in the soil of oppression. At midlife, there is still opportunity to make changes in what will become, in the end, the life that one has led. While, especially in ageist cultures (such as ours), all people may feel some pull toward a "younger" way of life, the desire to bask in a world that is less shaped by oppression can have a powerful lure for midlife lesbians.

Some of us will try to leave behind our history (and some of our oppression) and try to make a new, and perhaps better, life. The couple is implicated in this challenge. Some partners, like Lena, must risk the trust of her partner and the continuity of her couple relationship by finding part of herself outside herself. Other women may try to leave their past by leaving their partner. This strategy carries some of the gravest risk for life span development, because it may not be possible for these women, in the later part of life, to embrace fully all the years that have made their lives what they are.

Other midlife couples are more able to select, for themselves, from the smorgasbord of new options available to lesbian couples. For example, lesbian families have sometimes begun adding "grandmothers of choice" to create extended "families of choice." Grandmothers of choice are older women who, though not biologically related to them, build an intergenerational closeness and commitment to a lesbian-parent family. This kind of uniquely gay/lesbian generativity, like the community-based political, artistic, and helping outreach that has long characterized the involvement of midlife lesbian couples in our own communities, is a way that midlife couples disentangle themselves from a history of oppression, while retaining and respecting the place of their own life span in the context of cultural history.

Talking about family–grandmothers, mothers, children–is one way to embody the midlife life space that powerfully embraces the loyalty to early influences, personal expansion and joy, and the wish to nurture new growth. I want to underscore, however, that the creative-generative urge, the drive for integration, and the wish to delight in the precious time remaining find voice in far more ways than through family relations–in art, spirit, and appreciation of the natural world, in the joy of doing things well, in mentoring, in humanitarian concerns, and in care for one's self and for whatever matters to that self (including one's couple relationship).

CONCLUSION

The Usefulness of a Life Span Developmental Perspective

This paper has attempted to show the importance, for mental health professionals, of taking an informed life span developmental perspective on work with midlife lesbian couples and the individuals whose lives come together to form them. I have brought together research, theory, and clinical example to reflect some of the diversity among lesbian couples at midlife. At the same time, I have tried to make clear that particular developmental themes, and typical manifestations of them, create patterns in the panorama.

In this paper I have described only couples where both women are in midlife and have been together a considerable number of years. Although I have not included examples to show this, I have found that a recognition of midlife issues and the centrality of life span developmental process is equally useful in assisting lesbian couples with marked age differences and in helping newer couples with midlife members who find themselves in difficulty.

While midlife development may seem to have only small and positive reverberations in the lives of most lesbian couples, for other lesbian couples the repercussions may be profound. I have come to strongly believe that, when midlife lesbian couples turn to gay and lesbian social services for help, we can be most useful if we see the impact that results from the conscious or unconscious recognition that the bloom is on the rose and that, like all flowers in the exquisite beauty of their full bloom, they will fade with time. Couples' capacity to put this recognition to good use allows them to continue to grow, making their lives and others' richer as they move forward through the life span.

REFERENCES

Carstensen, L., & Pasupathi, M. (1993). Women of a certain age. In S. Matteo (Ed.), *American women in the nineties: Today's critical issues.* Northeastern University Press.

Erikson, E. (1950). *Childhood and society.* New York: Norton.

Gould, R. (1978). *Transformations: Growth and change in adult life.* New York: Simon & Schuster.

Hornstein, G. (1986). The structuring of identity among midlife women as a function of their degree of involvement in employment. *Journal of Personality, 54,* 551-575.

Jaques, E. (1965). Death and the midlife crisis. *International Journal of Psychoanalysis, 46,* 502-514.

Jordan, J. (1986). The meaning of mutuality. *Work in progress, number 23.* Wellesley, MA: Stone Center Working Paper Series. (Reprinted from *Women's growth in connection*)

Jung, C. (1960). The stages of life. In *The structure and dynamics of the psyche, collected works* (Vol. 8). Princeton, NJ: Princeton University Press. (First German edition, 1931)

Martin, D., & Lyon, P. (1972/1991). *Lesbian/Woman.* Volcano, CA: Volcano Press.

Miller, J. B. (1986). What do we mean by relationships? *Work in progress, number 22.* Wellesley, MA: Stone Center Working Paper Series. (Reprinted from *Women's growth in connection*)

Mitchell, V., & Helson, R. (1990). Women's prime of life: Is it the 50's? *Psychology of Women Quarterly, 14,* 451-470.

Neugarten, B. (1964). *Personality in middle and late life.* New York: Atherton.

Schoonmaker, C. V. (1993). The aging lesbian: Bearing the burden of triple shame. *Women & Therapy, 14*(1/2), 21-32.

Slater, S., & Mencher, J. (1991). The lesbian family life cycle: A contextual approach. *American Journal of Orthopsychiatry, 61*(3), 372-382.

Stewart, A., & Gold-Steinberg, S. (1990). Midlife women's political consciousness: Case studies of psychosocial development and political commitment. *Psychology of Women Quarterly, 14,* 543-566.

Whitbourne, S. K. (1986). *Adult development.* New York: Praeger.

Wrightsman, A. (1988). *Personality development in adulthood.* Newbury Park, CA: Sage.

Filial Bereavement:
Midlife Lesbian Daughters
and Intersubjective Thoughts

Jeanette Gurevitch

SUMMARY. Loss of parents for midlife lesbians is discussed in the context of continued development in middle age. From an intersubjective point of view, comprehension of externality, the capacity for mutual recognition, the disruption and repair of recognition and affirmation of subjectivity and the agenic "I" color relationships with parents throughout life. In filial bereavement, there can be a resurgence of intersubjective development along with an easing of internalized homophobia. In recovery from loss, there are opportunities to make loving identifications that more fully

Jeanette Gurevitch, LCSW, is a psychotherapist in private practice in Berkeley and San Francisco. She has a special interest in the modification of clinical theory and practice to reflect a deeper understanding of lesbian and gay people. She is a former adjunct professor and supervisor at John F. Kennedy University, New College, and California School of Professional Psychology, Alameda, California. Ms. Gurevitch is a founding board member of Rainbow Adult Community Housing in San Francisco, a nonprofit organization creating affordable and safe housing for old lesbian, gay, bisexual, and transgender people.

The author would like to thank the many friends, colleagues, and patients who contributed to these thoughts by sharing their own experiences of loss and bereavement. She would especially like to thank Marcy Adelman for her patience and support. Judy Greene, Catherine Teare, Maggie Rochlin, and Esther Lang are all greatly appreciated for their thoughtful assistance in preparation of this paper.

Jeanette Gurevitch, LCSW, can be reached at 2955 Shattuck Avenue, Berkeley, CA 94705; e-mail address: JGLCSW@aol.com.

[Haworth co-indexing entry note]: "Filial Bereavement: Midlife Lesbian Daughters and Intersubjective Thoughts." Gurevitch, Jeanette. Co-published simultaneously in *Journal of Gay & Lesbian Social Services* (Harrington Park Press, an imprint of The Haworth Press, Inc.) Vol. 11, No. 2/3, 2000, pp. 49-76; and: *Midlife Lesbian Relationships: Friends, Lovers, Children, and Parents* (ed: Marcy R. Adelman) Harrington Park Press, an imprint of The Haworth Press, Inc., 2000, pp. 49-76. Single or multiple copies of this article are available for a fee from The Haworth Document Delivery Service [1-800-342-9678, 9:00 a.m. - 5:00 p.m. (EST). E-mail address: getinfo@haworthpressinc.com].

49

acknowledge externality and difference. *[Article copies available for a fee from The Haworth Document Delivery Service: 1-800-342-9678. E-mail address: <getinfo@haworthpressinc.com> Website: <http://www.haworthpressinc.com>]*

KEYWORDS. Lesbian, bereavement, parents, recognition, identification, death, homophobia, generativity, loss, midlife

She and her "spouse" cared for her mother in their home for the last year of her mother's life. Moments after her mother's death, she leaned over and whispered, "Mom, I never told you I was a lesbian."

–A friend

Each lesbian daughter's response to the loss of a parent is as unique as her own history. However, for lesbians as for others, loss of parents is a common milestone in midlife.[1] Recovery from bereavement can contribute to midlife development, just as midlife capacities shape the experience of filial bereavement. Successes in both recovery from filial bereavement and in midlife transitions require the capacity to acknowledge mortality and to tolerate deep losses in pursuit of a deeper subjectivity. At midlife, loss of a parent, however painful or relieving, exerts an influence on adult development (Chiroboga, 1982), amplifying and contributing to the unfolding of psychological changes in middle age (Moss & Moss, 1983; Scharlach, 1993). For lesbians, as for gay men, the realization of a more robust subjectivity-fuller authorship and ownership of one's life (Benjamin, 1988)–can ease internalized homophobia and support midlife generativity. This paper examines filial bereavement in the context of lesbian midlife development through an intersubjective lens.

A LESBIAN MIDLIFE

Midlife, itself, is framed by a profound shift in identity: from one of maturation, emphasizing "what I will be," to more certain ownership of "what I have been" and "what I am." The internal push toward consolidation of identity initiates a reevaluation of "what I have been" and spurs reworking of past developmental issues (Apter, 1995; Jacques, 1965; Moss, 1984). Vital preparation for the vulnerability of continued aging, the emerging emphasis on "what I am," deepens subjectivity. This emotional robustness is rooted in a new self-confidence and certainty (Apter, 1995) with reduced barriers to assertion. The deepening of subjectivity in midlife fosters an expanded sense of agency, the assertion of desire (Apter, 1995; Benjamin, 1988).

For lesbians and gay men in particular, a midlife review of achievements, strengths, regrets, disappointments, and challenges to self-worth is accompanied by a review of coming out and the amalgamation of sexual orientation into their lives (Fertitta, 1988; Kimmel & Sang, 1995). Evaluating the influence of sexual identity on one's life generates complex emotions. The generation of lesbians now in midlife[2] has experienced a painful clash between the ideals of authenticity and freedom and the realities of loss of heterosexual privilege. The visibility and political actions of this generation have offered a degree of insulation from family and societal expectations that support subjectivity and assertion. On the one hand, "coming out" is a deep expression of subjectivity, described by Burch (1997) as an amplification of differentiation: "In an internal sense, claiming homosexuality as an identity usually means differentiating or disidentifying from both parents. . . . An individual beginning to take on such an identity inevitably takes another step on the path of separation" (p. 39).

On the other hand, confrontation with stigma and the loss of social recognition can deplete the self and numb desire (Buloff & Osterman, 1985). This cohort acknowledges barriers and prejudices they have faced and makes a bittersweet comparison with the relative openness and ease experienced by younger lesbians. Embedded in "affirmation of the younger generation's right to unfold" (Kohut, 1982, p. 402), for midlife lesbians, is pride in their own generation's contributions. At midlife, lesbians (and others, particularly other women) face the differences in opportunity for subsequent generations and struggle to distinguish between the limits imposed by the historical times and those imposed by their own ambitions or talents. For this cohort of lesbians, a midlife review acknowledges many of the losses and gains normative to midlife along with the painful acceptance, once again, of the fear and limitations imposed by a stigmatized identity (Glassgold, 1995).

At midlife, we experience a resurgence of anxieties about safety and vitality (Jaques, 1965). For lesbians, these concerns can echo the anxieties of coming out, as they are faced, once again, with a developmental step for which there is no visible road map.[3] As one woman put it, "So, yes, now I notice my wrinkles and beginning gray hair and have debates in my head again for the first time since I was an adolescent about what it is to be 'normal'" (Turner, 1991, p. 63). These anxieties about "normalcy" have frequently been affirmed in each daughter's confusing experiences of recognition, rejection, and denial both in her family and outside. Schwartz (1998) aptly describes the confusing press towards inauthenticity posed by even benign familial heterophilia[4]–the assumption and overvaluing of heterosexuality–which is the predominant reality in most families of lesbian daughters:

> The multiple internalizations of pseudo-compliant interactions with significant others masks one's true self's impulses toward subjectivity and the flowering of desire until they are so well hidden that they threaten to disappear. (p. 160)

The significance of "coming out" throughout life, is its essential relationship to authenticity and to subjectivity: "Coming out, then, is about being real. Coming out is about maximizing the ability to experience and express authentic desire, intimacy, and subjectivity in whatever form that might take" (Schwartz, 1998, p. 160). Parents' response to this expression of their daughter's subjectivity depends on their ability to tolerate a profound difference. Parental ease reflects the level of success (Burch, 1997) in their own achievement of subjectivity and capacity for mutual recognition. Throughout life, homophobia and heterophilia create barriers to recognition between daughters and parents, leading to distance and sometimes estrangement. Thus, for many in this cohort, loss of parents will occur in a relationship where connection has been strained and at times collapsed as parents and daughters retreat from the challenge posed by the difference in sexual identity. By midlife, family responses to a daughter's lesbianism and the consequent expansion and/or depletion of a daughter's sense of self have become less volatile as both daughters and parents reach compromises, expectations accommodate to possibilities, and connection is reestablished or expanded. At the same time, by midlife a strengthened sense of self (Magee & Miller, 1997) has been honed through the exceptional experience of a lifetime of coming out (Adelman, 1991). It is often the benefits of coming out in innumerable other contexts that strengthen and increase confidence and allow the consolidation of separation (Magee & Miller, 1997), such that parents and daughters can be in a prolonged process of establishing mutual recognition and a degree of affirmation. In these numerous other victories, lesbians buffer the difficulty and internal consequences posed by the strain in mutuality with parents.

By midlife, a greater degree of acceptance between parents and daughters accommodates some degree of resolution to the coming out crisis. If there were a period of conflict or estrangement, it often has softened to allow increased connection and continuation of the relationship with more mutual and enthusiastic reengagement. Daughters are more assured within themselves and parents less threatened as they have aged and developed different psychic and relational concerns. A growing sense of internal peace, coupled with the awareness of mortality, focuses lesbian daughters on acceptance of painful constraints and enjoyment of a reconstructed relationship, no matter how limited, with her parents.

This newly constructed relationship rests on a degree of "disregarded homophobia" (Adelman, personal communication, 1998): the disregard of parents' attitudes toward lesbianism and the consequences to self-esteem and vitality. The often-unintentional homophobia and heterophilia of parents is often defensively internalized, subtly burdening the lesbian daughter's sense of self, to protect the continued connection between daughter and parents. After a parent's death, there is often a deep, internal response to disregarded homophobia that can echo through many dimensions of a daughter's life and psyche, particularly in confluence with a midlife press towards an expanded subjectivity.

FILIAL BEREAVEMENT

The death of parents, like aging, has been anticipated in the part of our psyche that stores our fears as if they were merely fantasies. By midlife, conscious recognition or experience of a parent's mortality is accompanied by a disturbing awareness of one's own "finitude" (Moss, 1984). This overlap of issues often brings midlife lesbians, as others, into therapy, and these concerns are often embedded in other reasons for seeking treatment (Guttman, 1991).

Filial bereavement, both in its aspect of mourning and in the internal changes that accompany loss, is shaped by the salience of both external relationships with parents (Umberson, 1994) and intrapsychic relationships. The ages of parents and daughters, the anticipation of loss, and the experiences of care giving influence the depth of abandonment and eventual acceptance of loss. Aspects of differentiation, especially the capacities for separation and for integration (Horowitz, 1980, 1984; Jacobs, 1987-88; Scharlach, 1991) are particularly influential in shaping reactions to loss, as are intersubjective capacities, especially the comprehension of externality and the capacity for mutual recognition.

Feelings of relief or lack of intense distress or depression at the death of a parent do not indicate detachment from this loss (Umberson, 1994; Wortman, 1997), nor do they mean that bereavement will not spur developmental changes. Loss of parents can be psychologically meaningful without being acutely distressing. Some daughters will experience relief and release at the ending of a difficult relationship where parental problems, such as alcoholism, abuse, or mental illness, have dominated. When parental homophobia or other failures of recognition have been especially painful and significant, there also may be feelings of release and a resurgence of development as internal barriers are eased.

As with any increase in psychic vulnerability, loss of a parent also presents risks to the self and to current relationships. The developmental potential of bereavement may be unrealized if a daughter does not have the internal resources to meet the challenge (Sacks, 1998; Guttman, 1991), or if disturbing experiences or depression overwhelm the developmental push initiated by filial bereavement (Kaltreider, 1984; Malinak, 1979; Moss & Moss, 1983-84; Sacks, 1998; Scharlach, 1993; Volkan, 1981). For example, internal object relationships may no longer be able to contain latent negative self-images, and dreaded views of the self may emerge into conscious awareness (Horowitz, 1980; Kaltreider, 1984). The emergence of earlier images of a too needy, selfish, or depleted self may displace stronger self-images. Filial bereavement challenges current relationships, which must meet the amplified and sometimes fundamentally changed needs of the bereaved. The compelling experiences and behaviors that accompany unconscious internal shifts can contribute to stressful and often confusing emotions and behaviors. For example, the bereaved may feel neglected or neglectful or be unable to acknowledge these feelings even when they match behaviors. The painful aspect of the real or symbolic relationship with a parent may press for expression in current relationships (Guttman, 1991; Kaltreider, 1984) or produce troubling identifications (Sacks, 1998), and the unconscious meanings of relationships may be altered to correspond to internal shifts. Relationships are frequently symbolically tested to determine if they can respond to these urgent or new needs (Kaltreider, 1984). Leah's story illustrates these themes.

Leah: Release

Leah's father died when she was in her early 50s, at a time when she was already actively reevaluating her life, especially her relationship with her partner of 15 years, MK. Although their relationship had been historically turbulent, Leah and MK had been surprisingly unengaged in conflict for the previous few years, more committed to repairing disruptions and accepting limitations. Leah's father's death, in his 80s, was a release that unexpectedly propelled her out of a passive acceptance of thwarted subjectivity and toward a freer assertion of desire.

Leah's father had offered little recognition to his daughter when she was younger, ignoring her competence and meeting her efforts to identify with him with competition and rejection. He greeted the news of her first professional job by saying, "What could you do that anyone would pay you that kind of money?" Leah responded in kind: she remembered thinking, when her son was born, "I could do something my father could not do–have a boy." By midlife, however, Leah's bitter rivalry with her father had long since quieted, fading into a mutual disengagement that had become a re-acknowledgement of each other.

Leah's parents had accepted her lesbian relationship without any of the enthusiasm they had shown for her earlier heterosexual marriage. For her father, Leah's major achievement was providing him with grandchildren, affirming that she had been successfully heterosexual. Leah, however, already had experienced the disturbing consequences of not being a "subject" in her attempts to remain in her heterosexual marriage and was fiercely protective of her right to her own life. Her parents' disinterest in her remained painful, but less acutely so than in earlier times, and the family had a friendly connection that was inclusive of MK.

After her father's death, Leah felt "suspended" and quite consciously "freed to be more myself." She deeply felt her father's loss and through her grief could reclaim her attachment to him. While her mourning was not especially painful, she was deeply preoccupied in reviewing and understanding their relationship and in healing the last of her repudiation of him. She experienced an end to her struggles with him and felt freed from fear of his anger and threatened abandonment. She felt stronger, as if she could "provoke something and make something happen–with a different resolution. I was released from useless effort."

Leah had accepted long ago the echoes of the competition with her father in her relationship with MK. MK's subtle coercion of Leah, and Leah's corresponding resistance or subsequent collapse into submission, mirrored the dynamic with her father. Leah hoped that MK would shift in response to her own internal expansion, her renewed confidence in self-assertion. Instead, only a month after her father's death, Leah left her partner of 15 years. In her own words, she:

> . . . broke up in order to be myself without the fight for recognition that I had always had. I knew that that aspect of my relationship with my father was over, he had acknowledged me as much and as little as he ever would, and I didn't need to fight that fight with anyone ever again. I knew that [my partner and I] couldn't relate any differently than we always had, but now I could really leave. I was through.

For Leah, her father's death lifted a burden that subtly had diminished her desires. At midlife, she had consciously settled into her relationship with MK, confident about managing its limitations and actively shaping her life to reflect more fully her own choices. Her father's death amplified her determination to have greater ownership of her life by releasing her into a deeper desire for mutuality–the experience of recognizing and being recognized by a loved outside other. While undeniably sad, Leah's "divorce" from MK did not engender an unbearable grief or anxiety, but rather a deepened ease and confidence in her own assertion.

The Intersubjective Lens

Intersubjective theory is particularly appropriate to a discussion about the loss of parents. When we lose a parent, we are affected both by the loss of our external relationship with that parent and by loss of that parent as an internal object. Although childhood developmental tasks substantially have been achieved by adulthood, living parents have a continuing influence on unconscious psychic life, and early developmental dynamics continue within a more mature psychology. Tyson (1983) describes the continuation of rapprochement to sustain both object and self-constancy in adulthood as "Some refueling from the real object is needed from time to time in order to maintain the corresponding mental representation; the real object serves to refuel the constant self as well" (p. 259). The intersubjective capacities-comprehension of externality, recognition, and subjectivity-we can assume require the same contribution. Living parents, even at midlife, remain influential intersubjectively as they are intrapsychically.

Benjamin's ideas (1988, 1990, 1991, 1995) about intersubjective development illuminate how filial bereavement is influenced by and influences both intrapsychic and intersubjective realities:

> By encompassing both dimensions, we can fulfill the intention of relational theories: to account both for the pervasive effects of human relationships on psychic development and for the equally ubiquitous effects of internal psychic mechanisms and fantasies in shaping psychological life and interaction. (Benjamin, 1990, p. 35)

In an intersubjective view, the internal psychic world, created through internalizations and fantasy, exists in tension with the pleasure of discovering, engaging, and connecting with-and simultaneously being discovered by-an outside, independent subject. Differentiation is reinterpreted (Benjamin, 1990) to include, along with the internalization of object constancy, establishment of the capacity for mutual recognition, in which the "subject gradually becomes able to recognize the other person's subjectivity, developing the capacity for attunement and tolerance of difference" (p. 33). In discovery of the external subject, and in apprehending oneself as "like subject" (Benjamin, 1995, p. 7), one becomes able to, and desires to, recognize others. The exchange of recognition affirms subjectivity. In the interplay between intrapsychic and relational worlds, "the balance *within* the self depends upon mutual recognition *between* self and other, and mutual recognition is perhaps the most vulnerable point in the process of differentiation" (Benjamin, 1988, p. 53).

This vulnerability is twofold. First, recognition itself is an unstable aspect of psychology that is deeply challenged by the intrapsychic processes of internalization. Second, recognition is never a stable achievement, but rather entails a sustained tension between its disruption and repair. Recognition oscillates between its negation, which generates internal psychic fantasy, and its assertion, which affirms shared reality. The acknowledgement of negation of recognition is critical to its repair. When negation occurs through collapse into defensive identifications that abrogate difference or loss, the challenge is to recover externality and connection. When negation occurs through the change wrought by influence, the oscillation back toward recognition is achieved through acknowledgement and acceptance of being changed. Thus, both the quality of mutual recognition and the ease of its disruption and repair shape subjectivity.

Failures in recognition burden and constrain subjectivity. The wish for a mutuality with parents that acknowledges difference, such as lesbianism, is deep and abiding. The primal attachment to parents creates a profound vulnerability to collapses of mutual recognition in this relationship. While normal disruptions with parents are reparable, more serious breakdowns may overwhelm capacities and seriously burden subjectivity. These collapses can color the filial relationship throughout life. When recognition cannot be adequately reestablished, the self's relation to the internal object dominates and restricts subjectivity.

Since Freud (1917/1994), theories of bereavement have focused on intrapsychic processes: the press to internalize aspects of the deceased in order to maintain an attachment to primary figures and stabilize the self. Initially, the difficulties wrought by both introjection and identification of an ambivalently, rather than positively, held other were understood to be an attribute of "melancholia" or "pathological grief" (Freud, 1917/1994). Abraham (1927/1994) expanded this view and described internalizations, both introjection and identification, as central to all bereavement. Continuing this trend, modern theorists acknowledge the universality of ambivalence in all relationships. Even when filial bereavement is uncomplicated, many of the overwhelming emotions and psychological dynamics of more complicated grief are present, with muted and less disturbing intensity (Hartz, 1986; Horowitz, 1981; Jacobs, 1987-88; Kauffman, 1993-94; Moss, 1983-84; Prigerson, Frank, Kasl, Reynolds, Anderson, Zubenko, Houck, George, & Kupfer, 1995; Scharlach, 1991; Zisook, 1983).

Horowitz (1980, 1990) illustrates the consequence in filial bereavement of earlier collapses in mutual recognition that were not available for repair. He writes that disruption of a relationship where the self was experienced as positive or strong, and deflated self-images were denied, was the catalyst for tremendous psychic disturbance consequent to loss of a parent. Rather than introjection of an ambivalently held other, "a major cause of pathological grief appears to be the re-emergence of earlier self-images and role relationship models. These were established before the loss but were held in check by a more positive relationship" (Horowitz, 1980, p. 1159). In Eileen's story, the achievement of "self as subject" buffered earlier difficulties that re-emerged consequent to loss of her father.

Eileen: Collapse

Eileen, 45, was the favored daughter of a possessive, frustrated, and bitter father. Eileen was forced by her father's endless needs into a truncated mutuality where her own desires and disappointments went unacknowledged and she felt coerced into her acknowledgement of him. His desire for engagement dominated their relationship. Her father had responded to her disclosure of her sexual identity with characteristic intrusiveness–he pursued friendships with lesbians and boasted about lesbians' acceptance of him. Eileen and her father were locked in a struggle:

> He wanted into my life in a way that I did not want him. I never found a place of comfort with him as a child or an adult, always struggling with how much to see him, how to see him. I always felt conflicted, never felt right. He was highly intelligent and verbal, should have been something, a teacher or a minister. He had too much need, too much desire, too much demand–there was never a way to be comfortable with him.

During her earlier adult years, Eileen had accepted the extreme limitations of her relationship with her father and felt positive about her assertion and her success in shaping their relationship to reflect her own needs for both contact and separation.

Upon his death, Eileen's grief was mixed with profound relief. A month later she was flooded by an intensity of feeling she previously had not known: "His death pushed me down into small parts of myself, wounded, unsafe, broken self-esteem, hatred of him, acute guilt and discomfort about never loving him enough." After her father's death, stimulated by the internal contemplation of their relationship, she tumbled into the "small parts of her" that were overburdened both by internal psychic fantasy and by identification with parts of her father. Unlike the stronger parts of her psychology, these aspects of her psyche had been unavailable for refinement in oscillations with inter-subjective experience. These ossified parts emerged, painfully small and disturbed by the experience with her father. In this painful and depleted state, external realities did not offer a trustworthy contrast to the drama of internal objects. She was blocked from the reparative, intersubjective sequence of assertion, recognition, and subjectivity. Her inner world of fantasy was unbalanced, and her intersubjective resources for dissolving aggression (towards others or towards the self) were unavailable to mediate her experiences of rage and guilt.

The collapse of intersubjective space is a common feature of filial bereavement, but it generally appears in more muted fashion in Ei-leen's case. Bereavement challenges, as happened to Eileen, the bal-ance between intersubjective and intrapsychic images. The psychic imperative to internalize a deceased parent–the press toward identifi-cation and introjection–further threatens this balance. In introjection, the object is incorporated without the melding of object representation into self-representation and takes such forms as symptoms, internal regulations, and ideation. What is introjected can be projected outward onto persons or objects in the environment–as in transferences–or on to what Volkan terms "linking objects" (Klass, 1987-88), which sym-bolize important attributes of the deceased. When object representa-tions are modified to resemble self-representations in identification, the effort to maintain connection to the lost object can be enriching. Paradoxically, Volkan (1981) points out, identification also opens the way for independence from the object, for "when the self and model are perceived as one, relative independence from the original model is achieved" (p. 70).

In Benjamin's theory (1988, 1990, 1995, 1998), relative indepen-dence–an attribute of subjectivity–is maintained by balance in the oscillation between identification and recognition. Identification poses inevitable challenges to recognition. As Benjamin states, " . . . we are captive to identification, for recognition inevitably takes the indirect and potentially alienating form of identification, in which self takes the other as ideal or as a part of self, thus abrogating difference and externality" (1998, p. 95). In the negation of recognition, the intrapsychic landscape and dynamics of internalization dominate our experience. In the intrapsychic world, identifications can pose difficulties. Without the balance of recognition, identifications can be coercion to become the other or to abrogate externality and difference by creating merger, false unity, or splitting, or they defensively can deny differences or commonalties through idealizations or repudiations. When identification and introjection exist in tension with recognition, forming the oscillations between recognition and negation, then bereavement can acknowledge difference, facilitating both the acquisition and loosening of identifications with the deceased.

Fundamental to the capacity for mutual recognition is the comprehension of externality, which is crucial to mediating the challenge of identification. Out of the interplay, in early development, between the fantasized, aggressive destruction of the other and their real survival, the externality of the other becomes established. When the object survives the fantasized destruction, a "subject" with an independent center of being—an external being like oneself—is discovered, and one's own "subjectness" is affirmed. In the pleasure of this discovery, we not only desire recognition but also become able to, and wish to, recognize others. When externality is established:

> Identification can serve as a means for bridging difference without denying or abrogating it, but the condition of this form of identification is precisely the other's externality. . . . It is here that the notion of recognition as mediated not only through identification, but through direct confrontation with the other's externality, makes a difference. (Benjamin, 1998, p. 95)

In this context, the intrapsychic difficulties of coercion and domination posed by identification and introjection of a deceased parent can be mediated by the comprehension of externality that supports recognition of subjectivity and independence.

Klein and Volkan both have described a disturbance in the internal world as characteristic of bereavement. For Klein, loss is elaborated intrapsychically in disturbed object relations. This disturbance stems from the unconscious fear that because the loved one is gone, internal good objects are gone as well. Enrichment of the self in mourning happens through reinstatement and deepening of the relationship with the good internal objects by "recovering what had already [been] attained in childhood" (1940, p. 113). When, for midlife adults, loss of a parent is experienced as a substantiation of externality, Benjamin (1990) would draw an important distinction from Klein. Parallel to earlier development, the outcome of bereavement "is not simply reparation or restoration of the good object, but love, the sense of discovering the other" (p. 41). In the balance between recognition and identification, it is establishment of continuing ties to the deceased parent, rather than detachment (Abraham, 1927/1994; Freud, 1917/1994), that resolves bereavement (Moss, 1993; Valiant 1985). Volkan (1981) broadens Klein's view of the disturbance in the internal world engendered by loss of parents and emphasizes the actual reworking of developmental issues. He states that "the death of a loved one precipitates the hypercathexis of the representation of the dead, reviving old conflicts among self and object relationships" (p. 15). Mourning, in Volkan's view, demands "new inner adjustments to restore the previously established, newly disturbed balance among them" (1981, p. 15). Upon loss of a parent, the moorings of internal psychological constructs–purposeful, defensive, expressive, reparative, expansive, and adaptive–are temporarily less anchored and more available for new compromise formations.

Death ends parental refueling and requires withstanding the absolute loss of the outside other. Daughters must now survive the dissolution of primary biological bonds and recognize this destruction as profound externality rather than overwhelming abandonment. In whatever degree the arena for the "catching and throwing" of recognition (Benjamin, 1998, p. 29) has been established, it is now a new playing field. There is the opportunity to shape, and even a press to alter, psychological capacities, as they are disrupted and repaired without parental contribution in a more absolute comprehension of externality.

Sally's therapy was a reparative journey toward a resurgence of intersubjective development and reworking of identifications subsequent to the deaths of her mother and then her father. The achievement of a more substantial externality and capacity for recognition came out of her journey to rediscover, and, in a sense, recover, her parents and herself.

Sally: Recognition and Identification

At age 46, Sally, a managing scientist, was referred to me when her mother was diagnosed with terminal cancer. She had been in therapy in the past, but she had only pursued brief treatments. In the confluence of her mother's diagnosis and her own midlife, she was more committed to withstanding disappointments than she had been in previous therapies. As she faced her mother's death, she feared being either overwhelmed with anxiety or the opposite–experiencing an absence of emotion, a familiar feeling of her own "deadness."

Sally was devoted to her mother. Her attachment to her mother was characterized by a persistent anxiety. Sally had been a year old when her mother was hospitalized for many months with a "nervous breakdown," and for the rest of her life, Sally's mother suffered from a chronic mental disorder with agoraphobic features. In Sally's fantasy of these events, her mother had been unable to fully survive Sally's "aliveness." Her mother did survive, but her continuing frailty offered a weakened externality that made it difficult for Sally to develop a balance between internal fantasies and shared reality. In a fragment of omnipotent fantasy, Sally believed that her mother "was held captive by my grandmother and father. They saw only her fragility, not her strengths. She was always getting stronger, preparing to have more of a life (with me)." Sally was convinced of her own, essential role in her mother's survival:

I would never fight with my mother; she let me do as I pleased, but I was always "good," as I didn't want to harm her or make her upset. I remember once when I was sick and threw up, my mother wringing her hands and crying. I felt afraid and awful for her, and I always tried to avoid making her worry.

With limited trust in her mother's independent subjectivity, as well as her own, Sally had little confidence in her ability to dissipate difficult emotions through relating. Without a clearly established externality, confrontation with conflict or difference posed a problem: what to do with bad feelings? To avoid this dilemma, Sally prohibited herself from assertion. She hid differences from her family, keeping secret both difficulties and successes. By adolescence, she thought of herself as living a secret but successful life.

Although her mother's burdened survival engendered a compromised externality, there was still, between them, the joy of discovery and love (Eigen, 1981; Ghent, 1990). Her avoidance of difficulties was an attempt, albeit a costly one for her, to protect and nourish their connection. Despite her mother's dependence and fragility, Sally had an intrinsic sense of her mother's "subjectness" (Chodorow, 1979) upon which to base her own subjectivity. Sally's passionate relationship with her mother also contributed to her development of subjectivity. For Sally, the relationship with her mother was a romance in which she rescued her mother, who was the desirable and entrapped other. Sally's mother welcomed her as the "stronger" one and encouraged her exploration of the world outside the family. While her mother's diminished subjectivity impeded Sally's development, her mother's acknowledgement of difference, her enthusiastic admiration, and her recognition of Sally's real competence contributed to the development of Sally's subjectivity–her real, though somewhat burdened, ability to act on her own desires and to engage in mutual recognition.

Sally felt very guilty about her revulsion toward her father but was angry with him for his controlling, dominating behavior and his escalating alcoholism. As a young girl, she had adored him, even though he was demanding and exacting. Early in life, she had been excited to be like him, loving hiking, boats, and being physical and strong. She thought of herself as the "daughter-son" for both of her parents. As an older child, she felt him withdraw, and she felt that he was no longer interested in her company but only in her "performance." In latency, she was even more determined and more rejected in her wish to be his "buddy." At his rejection, she began to feel a boiling anger toward him and an unconscious depletion.

Sally believed that, for her father, her lesbianism was a blow to their relationship: he was deeply disappointed in her and withdrew in quiet repudiation. Although he had been cordial to Ellen, her partner of eight years, he never spoke to Sally directly about his views on sexual identity, nor acknowledged the nature of her relationships. She believed that he could not relate to her as an adult lesbian:[5]

> He just cannot see me in any way, so I am invisible except if he is worried about my safety. Even though we both like and own boats, he takes no pleasure in this; in fact, he seems to resent that I think I can have a boat. He is angry about anything that I like that is his.

Although she had intense, internal relationships with both her parents, her other relationships were characterized by lack of intensity or expression of emotion. In our early sessions, Sally's "deadness" was palpable, and our connection and interaction would languish. Internally, she carefully monitored our relationship and was preoccupied with protecting herself from deep feeling, hers or mine. She warded off her jealousy and rivalry by finding numerous ways to mention my having other patients. She avoided or denied moments in which she "did not know" to insulate herself from domination. She was vigilant about my office, mentioning any small change in furnishings or placement of objects, thus on a fantasy level reassuring herself of my predictability and her safety in "knowing."

After some time, and numerous, somewhat truncated conversations, I suggested to Sally that, for her, the connection between us was filled with fantasized dangers and that she was making great efforts to protect us. I came to understand that Sally grappled with the dangers posed by others and by her own vulnerability with a paucity of language with which to express her emotions or inner life. She wanted me to protect her from going in some unarticulated "wrong direction." The prospect of relationship and collaboration, of revealing herself by reaching out, evoked fears of domination and suffocation. At the same time, her desires for recognition and engagement were revealed in her prolific, wry storytelling. Sally used her humor to both ward off my interpretations and to evoke spontaneous responses and laughter. She wanted to have an effect on me, not only to elicit the thoughtfulness of therapy but also a shared enjoyment and recognition of her in laughter. In these exchanges, she affirmed her existence and mine and was assuredly co-creator of the intersubjective space in the therapy.

In our conversations, Sally became aware that she feared both that the agony of dying would crush her mother long before her actual death, and that she would fail to protect her mother and be crushed herself. Sally was stunned and relieved that her mother spoke quite frankly about her life, her illness, and her feelings about death. "We had conversations that were painful and so honest, I never saw my mother be so strong." Seeing her mother being both fearful and accepting of dying touched Sally profoundly, but she felt uncomfortable in her feelings of relief and happiness when her mother was so ill. We explored this flood of good feeling to discover and deepen its meaning for Sally. Sally's mother's unexpected strength in facing death affirmed, for Sally, that her mother could emotionally survive the aggressive assault of her cancer. Her mother's emotional resilience confirmed her subjectivity. This newfound reality, that her mother could be external to and different from Sally's internal mother, both deepened Sally's experience of love and allowed her to feel more "alive." She felt released from her fear of "deadness," and her grief was now both painful and affirming of externality and recognition.

In a way common to people faced with losing a parent, Sally's own subjectivity seemed to deepen each week. She had a joyful determination to engage in mutual recognition in therapy, and she shared thoughts, emotions, and memories more easily. Out of the realization of safety in assertion came a resurgence of desire. Sally was determined to address the image of herself as submissive, particularly with her partner, Ellen, by "establishing a shared reality in which she would have a sense of agency and impact" (Benjamin, 1995, p. 92). Sally's wishes for mutual recognition, where she was recognized and where her recognition was accepted, posed a painful confrontation with Ellen's internalized homophobia. Ellen had not accepted Sally's family as her in-laws, although family was important to her, and had little interest in visiting Sally's mother or being involved in her dying. She also refused to acknowledge her relationship with Sally in her own family. For eight years, Sally had remained "a friend."

As Sally moved closer to the loss of her mother, she became anguished about being closeted in Ellen's family. "I am nothing to them, and they will never know who I am or what I mean to them." Her previous acceptance of Ellen's reluctance to be visibly lesbian diminished. Sally was devastated by this rejection of her assertion of a wish for recognition. She feared that her relationship would never expand to support a further extension of "coming out" and that she would never again have a "family." This confirmed, for Sally, that her desires were dominated by the weaknesses of her partner and that her partner would be unable to recognize or love the more desiring part of her. She began to feel intensely "suffocated" and that all desire, sexual and other, was smothered–and she felt the return of the familiar "deadness."

At this juncture, Sally and I had a crisis. She left Ellen but lied to me about this for several months–appearing to be with Ellen, while actually separated from her and beginning to date Grace. The confession of the lie, months later, was unconscious: Sally mentioned her anniversary with Grace. I was surprised and felt uncomfortable and betrayed.

Sally was deeply ashamed, and a bit gleeful. I had to struggle not to hide my distress and to assure Sally that I was not damaged and that we could both survive this and understand it. As we discussed Sally's deceit, she told me that she imagined that I would prefer her to stay with Ellen. She was unsure that I would accept her destruction of her relationship with Ellen. Could I support her desire for Grace if it meant the dissolution of her relationship with Ellen and, in her fantasy, the destruction of Ellen? Was my acceptance conditional on some constraint or "good way" to achieve what she wanted? Did my needs, as a therapist, for her life to go well (so I would not fail) outweigh my recognition of her? Would my anger devastate her? Among the many meanings of this transference enactment, what was persistently important was that our therapy relationship survived her deceit–an outcome that surprised Sally. During this storm of emotion, she finalized the end of her relationship with Ellen and her mother died. It was an extremely disrupted and saddened year, but it allowed the emergence of a strengthened subjectivity.

Six months after her mother's death, Sally's father was diagnosed with cancer and died, suddenly, the next month. As she was sorting through the vast collection of letters, ledgers, and pictures saved by her father, she was stunned to find several packages of love letters between her parents. In reading the letters and other memorabilia, Sally came to know her father as a person, a young man in love, a devoted son, an interesting correspondent, a young father. She re-found aspects of her father long buried and the opportunity to ask the questions, "Who were you, who are you in me, who am I to you, who am I?"

After her parents' deaths, Sally lived, for a while, as if her parents were still there: offering their approval or disapproval, accompanying her into her life as they had never done in reality. She pursued things that they had done, looked at boats, fished, traveled to places they wanted to visit but never could, and often daydreamed about what it would be like if they could be with her. She was fascinated with where to put what she had kept of theirs, engaged in pleasing them and not pleasing them, much as Volkan has described the use of "linking objects" to maintain a connection to the deceased. Her sessions began with questions about what they would have thought about both big and small events in her life.

In therapy, Sally reconstructed her experience with her parents and began to see them as outside others with their own concerns and difficulties. She also recognized she had not really known their relationship to each other. She discovered them as people struggling with an illness they did not understand and had certainly not expected. She became able to appreciate their devotion and strength and to mourn, in both anger and pain, the effects of their preoccupations on her. Her recognition of her parents, as a couple, apart from their parenthood of her, was an integral aspect of her mourning their deaths. As she began to recognize her parents as subjects, her involvement with their imaginary presence and their ownership of her life began to ease and a more comfortable attachment took its place. She was able to laugh when her inheritance paid for kitchen tile that both her parents would have disliked. In time, the items she had inherited no longer belonged to them; they became instead reminders of them.

As her recognition of her parents deepened, her introjections became identifications and were further refined in the intersubjective context of the therapy. In this refinement of her identifications over the next few years, she left her employment and ended her career as a scientist, a career that her father had shared. She returned to school and became a highly successful artist, acknowledging the influence of her mother's artistic hobbies, but far surpassing her mother's tentative footsteps. In her midlife, subsequent to the death of both parents, she experienced a resurgence of intersubjective development, a more robust subjectivity, and an easing of internalized homophobia.

Discussion

Sally's response to her parents' deaths was especially dramatic, filled with life changes that matched the shifts in her internal world and deepening intersubjective capacities. Before therapy and the loss of her parents, Sally's life had been severely constrained by a precarious comprehension of externality that erected barriers to assertion and the realization of subjectivity. Her relationships with each of her parents both contributed to her capacities for mutual recognition and agency, and to the fragility of these same capacities. Sally's mother supported her daughter's subjectivity and agency by accepting and enjoying the romance between them. Burch (1997) considers this shared romance to be a crucial substrate for the development of authenticity and wholeness, or subjectivity, of daughters. In Burch's view, the acceptance of her daughter's pre-oedipal and oedipal passion by her mother is intrinsic to her daughter's sense of agency and adequacy. Sally's father, in contrast to her weakened mother, was very much a "subject of desire," and his early direct recognition of her, as well as his acceptance of her symbolic identification with him (Benjamin, 1995, p. 122), also supported her sense of agency and subjectivity.

Identification, in reaching outward, rather than standing in negation to recognition, births the desiring subject–an agent. It is this agentic "I" that seeks the duality of identification, loving the other as fantasy object with the wish to assimilate what is other into the self, while engaging in mutual recognition with that external object. The realization of identificatory love is through both its elaboration in fantasy and its desire to be like the outside other. This duality expands intrapsychic representations of the self and also affirms the self as subject when the wish to "be like" is welcomed by the external other, as it was by Sally's father. This affirmed Sally as an agent, able to act upon and be recognized by other subjects. This aspect of subjectivity, Sally's agency, had been expressed further in her leaving home and in her "coming out" as a lesbian. Sally's "agentic I" held the multiple tensions between recognition and negation, between independence and influence, and between intersubjective and intrapsychic realities (Benjamin, 1990, 1995; Pollack, 1998) so that she could survive, as well as she did, her difficulties with her parents and their deaths.

Prior to her parents' deaths, Sally's own capacity for mutual recognition did not demand the reworking of either the false unity with her mother or the repudiation of commonality with her father. In therapy, acknowledging her mother's real limitations, and their impact on her, challenged Sally's idealizations and false closure of contradictions. This opened the door to identifications with her mother in which Sally remained a subject with differences from as well as commonalties with her mother. Identifications could then be expansive without abrogating difference, and she could feel distinct from her mother without denying attachment.

When the realization of mutual recognition is not "good enough," as between Sally and her parents, subjectivity is diminished, and negations of recognition are denied or experienced as destruction. In this context, identifications can be experienced as coercive commands. With her father, especially, Sally feared this internal coercion and was adamant in her conscious refusal: "I am not like them!" Her conscious repudiation of her father had been, in her estimation, a guard against domination. As her subjectivity deepened in therapy and in bereavement, unconscious identifications became available to be reworked in the therapy and Sally discovered that she was more like her father than she had recognized. Her discomfort with this was balanced by her deepening sense of emotional robustness. As her capacity for recognition deepened, these identifications, as well, became refined in the balance with recognition.

As her own intersubjective capacities became more robust, in therapy and with her mother, Sally came to desire recognition and to risk assertion. It is not surprising that Sally's desire was for recognition as a lesbian. Certainly, to be acknowledged as a lesbian daughter, daughter-in-law, partner, and lover is intrinsic to a lesbian's subjectivity. For Sally, a primary lesbian who felt her sexuality to be a given rather than a choice, and whose entire romantic and erotic life had been lesbian (Burch, 1993, p. 33), this desire for recognition was essential. The fulfillment of this desire continued, after her parent's death, to fuel her vitality and assertion of self. She could heal from her father's rejection of her lesbianism by recognizing the narrowness of his views and deepening her own visibility for herself. She confronted her fears and "came out," for the first time, at work, and in Grace's family. Sally's resolve to be more visible pushed her toward generativity as she revived and deepened old friendships that she had dropped when she "came out," and she also made new connections.

In the overlap of her own midlife and her parents' deaths, Sally was deeply engaged in a review of her life. "What I have been" became intertwined with "How am I like them?" The consolidation of "What I am" became intertwined with her new, mature recognition of her parents. Supported by my recognition of her, she could relinquish the repudiation of her father and the false sameness with her mother. Consolidation of identity, amplified by the loss of her parents, continued to deepen Sally's subjectivity and strengthen her assertion of desire. She developed a deeper capacity for mutual recognition with confidence in repair of its disruption.

CONCLUSION

For lesbians at midlife, loss of a parent can amplify the press for consolidation of a more robust subjectivity, the easing of internalized

homophobia, and the movement towards generativity. A midlife consolidation of identity for lesbians, as for others, is accompanied by an
inner confidence and acceptance, with increasing involvement in generative extensions–the purposeful extension of self to others as well as
to oneself in further identity development (Erikson, 1985). Schwartz
(1998) describes the relationship between internalized homophobia
and generativity:

> The denigration and/or repression of desire has a direct and re-
> pressive effect on the agentic functions of one who produces or
> creates. Moreover, what is there to "pass on" within a genera-
> tional context, if what one *is* feels contaminated, tainted by the
> culturally constructed abjectness of the lesbian self? (p. 96)

Thus, with the easing of internalized homophobia and the emergence,
in midlife, of an empowered sense of agency and subjectivity, generativity can emerge to provide unity, purpose, and meaning to life (Mc-
Adams & St. Aubin, 1992).

By midlife, the survivals of stigma and rage, and the experiences of
disruption and repair, have strengthened the agentic "I" and capacities
for recognition and tolerance of difference. A more robust capacity for
mutual recognition fosters ease in the oscillations between recognition
and negation. There is trust in and capacity for recognition, rather than
false closure of contradiction. Trust in externality and mutuality that
was challenged by the revelation of sexual orientation has been repaired. With loss of parents, identifications are newly available for
renegotiation and refinement in the disruption and repair of mutual
recognition.

As aging progresses, successes in the continuous repair of disruptions to recognition strengthen the capacity to recognize and deepen
mutuality, calming the acuteness of oscillations in a more complete
recognition.

> Recognizing the other happens when we are required to go a
> step beyond this mere commonality or identification to work
> through our differences with the other, arriving hopefully (but
> never finally) at the simultaneity of commonality and differ-
> ence. Perhaps the point is that, once we get to that simultaneity,
> the struggle takes on a less "life-and-death" quality. (Benjamin,
> 1999, p. 398)

Through the repair of disruption and achievement of a balance between negating externality in the service of intrapsychic process and recognizing externality in the repair of mutuality, both intrapsychic and intersubjective aspects of the psyche are enriched. In filial bereavement, these more robust intersubjective capacities support new opportunities to make identifications that acknowledge both externality and difference. The challenge, in bereavement, is to hold mutual recognition and self-as-subject without the parental contribution and gently repair the collapse into defensive identifications or denials which abrogate loss.

NOTES

1. By age 54, 50% of children have lost at least one parent, and by age 62, 75% have lost both parents (Winsborough, 1991).

2. The cohort of lesbians now in midlife is the first and last generation to have lived their adolescence and young adulthood in hiding and their adulthood, since the 1970s, with an increasingly public community. Through their political, professional, and community actions, the boomer generation of lesbians and gay men, with others, has lived and shaped an historical time in which lesbians, as a group, have achieved more visibility and acceptance so that each subsequent generation of lesbians will live with fewer barriers. Young lesbian professionals can, now, look to other "out" lesbian professionals for guidance and support. Lesbian and gay employee associations exist within many large companies. That lesbians can ascertain the identity of other lesbians without great difficulty is a remarkable difference. Heterosexual parents of lesbians can anticipate grandchildren outside of a heterosexual coupling. Lesbians of succeeding cohorts will experience fewer barriers to all forms of generativity as they reach midlife. Lesbian experience can, now, range from the loss of children and jobs across the spectrum of discrimination to the opposite experience of being "out" as the CEO of major corporations. Within this range of possibilities, while there is still a long way to go, the differences for a younger cohort of lesbians, particularly in urban areas, are stunning.

3. For this cohort of lesbians, like others with partially or wholly hidden lives, there is a paucity of visible elders to provide models of aged life that suggest continuity and survival. The quality of filial bonds and the differences in lifestyle and lifestyle solutions diminish the support from family models of aging. The older cohort of gays and lesbians has remained more closeted in their lives and hidden in their aging. This may generate increased anxiety for midlife lesbians as the rules and roles available in younger life provide less and less structure for the developmental tasks (generativity, ego-integrity, and wisdom) of midlife and aging.

4. D. Schwartz (1993) makes a poignant distinction between homophobia and heterophilia, "the overvaluing of intimate relationships between different sexed partners" (p. 643). In filial relationships that grow to include warmth and acceptance of a daughter's lesbianism and others that do not rest on outright devaluation of lesbian-

ism, there is still the expression of heterophilia "including the idealization of its contemporary practices, parenthood and state-sanctioned marriage" (p. 648). In filial relationships, this devaluation is often expressed in parent's awkwardness in relating to their daughter's life and her relationships, the lack of interest in her community and its culture, and the resistance towards being inclusive and protective of important people in her life. This attitude exists, often in sharp contrast to their excitement and celebration of heterosexual milestones, and continuing interest in all aspects–large and small–of heterosexual life.

5. Hansell (1998) speculates about the unconscious relationship of men to women that relies on rigid complementarities of gender. In her lesbianism, her sense of herself without men, Sally refused, in the unconscious relationship between her and her father, to be the repository of his split-off femininity and to support his esteem by acquiescing to his dominance. His withdrawal of mutual recognition was an expression of his own difficulties, as well as of his covert hostility. In the collapse of intersubjective space in the relationship, without repair, the complementarity of dominance and submission added fuel to Sally's subtly submissive passivity in relationships and her intense anger toward her father.

REFERENCES

Abraham, K. (1994). A short study on the development of the libido. In R. V. Frankiel (Ed.), *Essential papers on object loss* (pp. 72-93). New York: New York University Press. (Original work published 1927)

Adelman, M. (1991). Stigma, gay lifestyles, and adjustment to aging: A study of later-life gay men and lesbians. In J. S. Lee (Ed.), *Gay midlife and maturity* (pp. 7-32). New York: The Haworth Press, Inc.

Apter, T. (1995). *Secret paths: Women in the new midlife.* New York: Norton.

Benjamin, J. (1988). *The bonds of love.* New York: Pantheon Books.

Benjamin, J. (1990). An outline of intersubjectivity: The development of recognition. *Psychoanalytic Psychology (suppl),* 33-46.

Benjamin, J. (1991). Father and daughter: Identification with difference–A contribution to gender heterodoxy. *Psychoanalytic Dialogues, 1*(3), 277-299.

Benjamin, J. (1995). *Like subjects, love objects.* New Haven: Yale University Press.

Benjamin, J. (1998). *Shadow of the other: Intersubjectivity and gender in psychoanalysis.* New York: Routledge.

Benjamin, J. (1999). A note on the dialectic: Commentary on paper by Bruce E. Reis. *Psychoanalytic Dialogues, 9*(3), 395-399.

Buloff, B., & Osterman, M. (1995). Queer reflections mirroring and the lesbian experience of self. In J. Glassgold & S. Iasenza (Eds.), *Lesbians and psychoanalysis: Revolutions in theory and practice* (pp. 93-106). New York: Simon and Schuster.

Burch, B. (1993). *On intimate terms: The psychology of difference in lesbian relationships.* Urbana: University of Illinois Press.

Burch, B. (1997). *Other women: Lesbian/bisexual experience and psychoanalytic views of women.* New York: Columbia University Press.

Chiroboga, D. (1982). An examination of life events as possible antecedents to change. *Journal of Gerontology, 5,* 595-601.

Chodorow, N. (1994). Gender relations and difference in psychoanalytic perspective. In *Feminism and psychoanalytic theory.* New Haven: Yale University Press, 1989. (Original work published 1979)

Eigen, M. (1981). The area of faith in Winnicott, Lacan and Bion. *International Journal of Psychoanalysis, 62,* 413-433.

Erikson, E. (1985). *The life cycle completed: A review.* New York: W. W. Norton.

Fertitta, S. (1988). Never married women in the middle years: A comparison of lesbians and heterosexuals. Dissertation available through University Microfilms International.

Freud, S. (1994). Mourning and melancholia. In R. V. Frankiel (Ed.), *Essential papers on object loss* (pp. 38-51). New York: New York University Press. (Original work published 1917)

Ghent, E. (1990). Masochism, submission, surrender. *Contemporary Psychoanalysis, 26,* 169-211.

Glassgold, J. M. (1995). Psychoanalysis with lesbians: Self-reflection and agency. In J. Glassgold & S. Iasenza (Eds.), *Lesbians and psychoanalysis: Revolutions in theory and practice* (pp. 203-228). New York: Simon and Schuster.

Guttman, H. A. (1991). Parental death as a precipitant of marital conflict in middle age. *Journal of Marital and Family Therapy, 17*(1), 81-87.

Hansell, J. H. (1998). Gender anxiety, gender melancholia, gender perversion. *Psychoanalytic Dialogues: A Journal of Relational Perspectives, 8*(3), 337-351.

Hartz, G. W. (1986). Adult grief and its interface with mood disorder: Proposal of a new diagnosis of complicated bereavement. *Comprehensive Psychiatry, 27*(1), 60-64.

Horowitz, M. (1990). A model of mourning: Changes in scheme of self and others. *Journal of the American Psychoanalytical Association, 38,* 297-324.

Horowitz, M., Krupnick, J., Kaltreider, N., Wilner, N., Leong, A., & Marmar, C. (1981). Initial psychological responses to parental death. *Archives of General Psychiatry, 38,* 316-323.

Horowitz, M., Wilner, N., Marmar, C., & Krupnick, J. (1980). Pathological grief and the activation of latent self-images. *American Journal of Psychiatry, 137*(10), 1157-1980.

Horowitz, M., Wilner, N., Marmar, C., & Krupnick, J. (1984). Reaction to the death of a parent. *The Journal of Nervous and Mental Disease, 172,* 383-392.

Jacobs, S. C., Korsten, T. R., Kasl, S. V., Ostfeld, A. M., Berkman, L., & Charpentier, P. (1987-88). Attachment theory and multiple dimensions of grief. *OMEGA, 18*(1), 41-53.

Jaques E. (1965). Death and the mid-life crisis. *International Journal of Psychoanalysis, 46,* 502-514.

Kaltreider, N., Becker, T., & Horowitz, M. (1984). Relationship testing after the loss of a parent. *American Journal of Psychiatry, 141*(2), 243-246.

Kauffman, J. (1993-94). Dissociative functions in the normal mourning process. *OMEGA, 28*(1), 31-38.

Kimmel, D., & Sang, B. (1995). Lesbians and gay men in midlife. In A. R. D'augelli

& C. J. Patterson (Eds.), *Lesbian, gay and bisexual identities over the lifespan* (pp. 190-214). New York: Oxford University Press.

Klass, D. (1987-88). John Bowlby's model of grief and the problem of identification. *OMEGA, 18*(1), 13-32.

Klein, M. (1994). Mourning and its relation to manic depressive states. In R. V. Frankiel (Ed.), *Essential papers on object loss* (pp. 95-121). New York: New York University Press. (Original work published 1940)

Kohut, H. (1982). Introspection, empathy and the semi-circle of mental health. *International Journal of Psychoanalysis, 63,* 395-407.

Magee, M., & Miller, D. C. (1997). *Lesbian lives: Psychoanalytic narratives old and new.* New Jersey: The Analytic Press.

Malinak, D., Hoyt, M. F., & Patterson, V. (1979). Adults' reactions to the death of a parent: A preliminary study. *American Journal of Psychiatry, 136*(9), 1152-1156.

Margolies, L., Becker, M., & Jackson-Brewer, K. (1987). Internalized homophobia: Identifying and treating the oppressor within. In Boston Lesbian Psychologies Collective (Eds.), *Lesbian psychologies: Explorations and challenges* (pp. 220-241). Urbana: University of Illinois Press.

McAdams, D., & St. Aubin, E. (1992). A theory of generativity and its assessment through self-report, behavioral acts and narrative themes in autobiography. *Journal of Personality and Social Psychology, 62*(6), 1003-1015.

Moss, M., & Moss, S. (1983-84). The impact of parental death on middle aged children. *OMEGA, 14,* 65-71.

Moss, M., Moss, S., Rubinstein, R., & Resch, N. (1993). Impact of elderly mother's death on middle age daughters. *International Journal Aging and Human Development, 37*(1), 1-22.

Pollock, L., & Slavin, J. H. (1998). The struggle for recognition: Disruption and reintegration in the experience of agency. *Psychoanalytic Dialogues, 8*(6), 857-873.

Prigerson, H., Frank, E., Kasl, S.V., Reynolds, C., Anderson, B., Zubenko, G. S., Houck, P. R., George, C. J., & Kupfer, D. J. (1995). Complicated grief and bereavement-related depression as distinct disorders: Preliminary empirical validation in elderly bereaved spouses. *American Journal of Psychiatry, 152*(1), 22-30.

Sacks, A. M. (1998). Bereavement: A special disorder of object loss (a comparison of two cases). *Psychoanalytic Psychology, 15*(2), 213-229.

Scharlach, A. E. (1991). Factors associated with filial grief following the death of an elderly parent. *American Journal of Orthopsychiatry, 61*(2), 307-313.

Scharlach, A. E., & Fredriksen, K. I. (1993). Reactions to the death of a parent during midlife. *OMEGA, 27*(4), 307-319.

Schwartz, A. E. (1998). *Sexual subjects: Lesbians, gender and psychoanalysis.* New York: Routledge.

Schwartz, D. (1993). The love that dare not speak its aim. *Psychoanalytic Dialogues, 3*(4), 643-652.

Turner, S. (1991). Crisis of loss. In B. Sang, J. Warshow, & A. J. Smith (Eds.), *Lesbians at midlife: The creative transition* (pp. 60-64). San Francisco: Spinsters Book Company.

Tyson, R. L. (1994). Some narcissistic consequences of object loss: A developmental view. In R. V. Frankiel (Ed.), *Essential papers on object loss* (pp. 252-267). New York: New York University Press. (Original work published 1983)

Umberson, D., & Chen, M. D. (1994). Effects of parent's death on adult children: Relationship salience and reaction to loss. *American Sociological Review, 59,* 152-168.

Valiant, G. E. (1985). Loss as a metaphor for attachment. *The American Journal of Psychoanalysis, 45*(1), 59-67.

Volkan, V. D. (1981). *Linking objects and linking phenomena: A study of the forms, symptoms, metapsychology and therapy of complicated mourning.* New York: International Universities Press.

Volkan, V. D., & Josephthal, D. (1994). The treatment of established pathological mourners. In R. V. Frankiel (Ed.), *Essential papers on object loss* (pp. 299-323). New York: New York University Press. (Original work published 1980)

Winsborough, H. H., Bumpass, L., & Aquilino, W. S. (1991). *The death of parents and transition to old age.* (Working Paper 39). Madison, WI: Center for Demography and Ecology, University of Wisconsin.

Wortman, C. (1997, October). In Researcher questions the way society grieves. *The Monitor, publication of the American Psychological Association, 36.*

Zisook, S., & DeVaul, R. (1983). Grief, unresolved grief and depression. *Psychosomatics, 24*(3), 247-256.

Lesbian Dating and Courtship from Young Adulthood to Midlife

Suzanna Rose
Debra Zand

SUMMARY. Lesbian dating and courtship were explored based on interviews with 38 predominantly white lesbians (ages 22-63) representing young adult, adult, and midlife age groups. Friendship was found to be the most widely used courtship script across all age groups, followed by the sexually explicit and romance scripts, with friendship and romance scripts being preferred. Unique aspects of lesbian dating cited by participants included freedom from gender roles, heightened intimacy/friendship, the rapid pace of lesbian relationship development, and the effects of prejudice. Friendship was found to be differentiated from romance by two main criteria: emotional intensity and sexual energy or contact. Verbal declarations of interest and nonverbal behaviors were the primary means of communicating sexual attraction. Few lesbians adhered to traditional gender roles in dating, and those who reported assuming the feminine reactive role nevertheless rejected the traditional notion that women should limit sexual contact. Overall, midlife lesbians were more purposive in their dating and more free from gender roles. Specifically, they were more concerned about the "attachment-worthiness" of a prospective partner and were significantly more likely

---

Suzanna Rose, PhD, is Professor of Psychology and Women's Studies at the University of Missouri-St. Louis. Dr. Rose also is founder and director of the St. Louis Lesbian and Gay Anti-Violence Project, which documents homophobic hate crimes and provides counseling and referrals to victims. Debra Zand, PhD, is a Research Assistant Professor of Psychiatry at the University of Missouri-Columbia. She received her doctorate in clinical psychology in 1997 from the University of Missouri-St. Louis, where she began her research on lesbian relationships.

[Haworth co-indexing entry note]: "Lesbian Dating and Courtship from Young Adulthood to Midlife." Rose, Suzanna, and Debra Zand. Co-published simultaneously in *Journal of Gay & Lesbian Social Services* (Harrington Park Press, an imprint of The Haworth Press, Inc.) Vol. 11, No. 2/3, 2000, pp. 77-104; and: *Midlife Lesbian Relationships: Friends, Lovers, Children, and Parents* (ed: Marcy R. Adelman) Harrington Park Press, an imprint of The Haworth Press, Inc., 2000, pp. 77-104. Single or multiple copies of this article are available for a fee from The Haworth Document Delivery Service [1-800-342-9678, 9:00 a.m. - 5:00 p.m. (EST). E-mail address: getinfo@haworthpressinc.com].

than young adults to view dating as having a serious goal, to proceed at a rapid pace, to ask for a date, and to initiate physical intimacy. *[Article copies available for a fee from The Haworth Document Delivery Service: 1-800-342-9678. E-mail address: <getinfo@haworthpressinc.com> Website: <http://www.haworthpressinc.com>]*

KEYWORDS. Lesbian, midlife, friendship, dating, courtship, gender roles, intimacy, relationship development, sexual attraction

INTRODUCTION

The question, "What will we be?" is one of the most exciting, mysterious, and confusing aspects of dating and courtship among lesbians. Will the relationship that just has been initiated result in being lovers, partners, or friends, or some combination? Moreover, exactly how do lesbian relationships typically get initiated? Is dating a clearly defined concept, or is the establishment of contact usually more ambiguous in its intent? These questions are of considerable interest to lesbians. A great many advice and humor books and social commentaries have addressed these issues (e.g., Bechdel, 1997; Eisenbach, 1996; McDaniel, 1995), but a lack of empirical evidence on the topic has ensured that descriptions largely remain anecdotal or speculative.

Our intent in the present research was to provide an in-depth descriptive account of lesbian dating and courtship that would begin to close the gap in knowledge concerning lesbian relationship formation. We examined what courtship scripts lesbians had used in past relationships, how they defined lesbian dating and what was unique about it, and how romantic relations versus friendship were solicited and developed. Also evaluated were the extent to which lesbians adopted gender roles when dating and the impact previous lesbian and heterosexual dating experience had on behavior. Last, a qualitative post hoc analysis was conducted to determine whether developmental changes in views about courtship emerged among the three age groups of participants, including young adult, adult, and midlife lesbians.

Dating and Courtship Scripts

Contemporary (heterosexual) courtship typically relies on dating as a way to initiate romantic relationships (Bailey, 1988). Dating refers to informal interactions with no specific commitment or goal between two individuals with the implied intent of assessing each other's romantic potential (Cate & Lloyd, 1992; Laws & Schwartz, 1977). Although often the labels "dating" and "courtship" are used interchangeably, courtship is a term arising from an earlier era that refers to the system of searching for a mate with whom to make an emotional commitment and enter into a permanent marriage (Cate & Lloyd, 1992). A graduated series of dates is considered the first step to a serious romance (Modell, 1983). Once an exclusive pairing has been established, a couple may enter into a more formal courtship phase.

The extent to which lesbians follow patterns of heterosexual dating and courtship has not been established. That some lesbians date is obvious. Personal advertisements written by lesbians often expressly state an interest in dating. Likewise, lesbians who participated in research by Cini and Malafi (1991) and Klinkenberg and Rose (1994) were able to provide detailed descriptions of dating. However, others declined to participate because they had gotten involved with a friend and never dated. Thus, dating and courtship as they traditionally occur may not apply to lesbians.

Three courtship scripts that have been used by Rose, Zand, and Cini (1993) to describe lesbian couple formation include a romance, friendship, and sexually explicit script. A script refers to a set of stereotypical actions defined by cultural norms that serve as a guide for what feelings and behaviors should occur in a specific situation (Gagnon, 1977; Ginsberg, 1988). The lesbian romance script depicts emotional intimacy and sexual attraction as being intertwined in two women's attraction to each other. The relationship usually rapidly proceeds towards commitment. Dating may be one means of initiating a relationship, but it appears that the dating phase for lesbians may be very short or that a more serious courtship may be preferred from the beginning. For instance, Cini and Malafi (1991) found that by a fifth date, respondents reported being both sexually and emotionally involved and tended to regard themselves as a couple.

In the other two major patterns of lesbian courtship, the friendship script and the sexually explicit script, the components of emotional intimacy and sexual attraction hypothetically play out differently. Neither script requires dating for its initiation. The friendship script, believed to be the most common courtship script among lesbians, emphasizes emotional intimacy over sexuality. According to this script, two women become friends, fall in love, and establish a committed relationship with each other that may or may not be sexual, as in the case of lesbian Boston marriages (e.g., Rothblum & Brehony, 1993). In contrast, the sexually explicit script primarily focuses on sexuality and attraction; emotional intimacy is less important or may not even be present. In this script, two women who are physically attracted to each other purposefully initiate sexual contact with no implied goal of future commitment.

The most immediate questions raised by the preceding discussion are: What courtship scripts do lesbians actually use, and what script is most preferred? Related issues concern how lesbians define dating and whether lesbian dating has unique characteristics not associated with heterosexual models. These were addressed in the present research. In addition, the degree to which scripts may overlap may create ambiguity. The courtship scripts described above may not be as distinct in practice as in theory. The friendship script is one that is particularly confusing, because it is often difficult for lesbians to know whether an informal interaction with another woman is a date or a non-romantic friendship overture. What script is followed may be easier to discern in retrospect than during its enactment. If the pair becomes a couple, they later may tend to classify the interaction as a date/romance script; if not, it may be seen as just getting together as friends. The motives of the two women involved also might differ, with one assuming they are "just friends" and the other assuming it is a date. Or, scripts might be blended, with both friendship and romance as the goal. Lesbians place a high value on friendship and appear to act quickly to establish an intimate connection within the context of a dating relationship (Rose et al., 1993). Two questions raised by script ambiguity that also were explored in the present research concerned how lesbians distinguish friendship from romance and what rituals signal the progression of the relationship to a more serious level, such as from friendship or dating to commitment.

Gender Roles and Courtship

The impact of gender roles on lesbian courtship also was investigated in the present research. First, it was expected lesbians would use more indirect than direct means of communicating interest in a partner. Traditional gender roles prescribe that men initiate the relationship; women are expected to wait to be asked for a date. As women, lesbians may not have been socialized to initiate dating or courtship. This is perhaps one reason lesbians have been described as notoriously inactive in approaching another woman in whom they are interested (e.g., DeLaria, 1995; Sausser, 1990) For instance, Jacqueline Lapidus (1995) labeled the non-initiating style of lesbian dating she practiced "procrasti-dating." In addition, although the direct initiation of contact in heterosexual interactions is traditionally the man's prerogative, research on nonverbal behavior indicates that women actually may do the choosing by signaling a partner to approach them using "proceptive behaviors" such as a darting glance, moving close, or touching (e.g., Perper & Weis, 1987; Moore, 1985). What is perceived as male choice may be, in fact, the final step of a selection and artful solicitation by the woman using eye contact, positive facial expressions, smiling, laughing, and light touch. Thus, as women, lesbians may be especially skilled at sending and interpreting nonverbal cues. Subsequently, we predicted that lesbians would rely on nonverbal proceptive behaviors more than direct verbal approaches (e.g., asking for a date) to convey romantic interest.

Second, based on gender socialization, we predicted that lesbians would prefer the friendship script over the romance or sexually explicit scripts. For instance, the need for one woman to assume the traditional male role of initiator in dating relationships may be circumvented by the friendship script. Women also generally are socialized to value intimacy and expressiveness over sexuality in relationships, a pattern of interaction that is most compatible with the friendship script. Moreover, the process of coming out occurs within the context of a friendship for many lesbians (e.g., Grammick, 1984).

Third, although heterosexuals' dating scripts have been shown to adhere strongly to gender roles, particularly among experienced daters, with men assuming an active role and women a reactive one (Rose & Frieze, 1989; 1993), lesbians were not expected to follow suit. When dating, lesbians tend not to assign the active role to one person, instead preferring to share the responsibility for orchestrating the date (Klinkenberg & Rose, 1994). In other words, lesbians typically behave consistently with gender roles, that is, most do not adopt the male role. The prediction that few lesbians would adopt heterosexual roles was explored in the present research by asking participants the extent to which they assumed either a traditional masculine role when dating (i.e., asking for a date, planning it, picking her up, performing courtly behaviors such as holding doors open, paying for the date, and initiating sexual contact), or a feminine role (i.e., waiting to be asked for a date, and allowing or refusing sexual advances). Previous heterosexual and lesbian dating experience also was assessed in order to test whether dating experience affected gender role behavior.

In summary, it appears that an exploration of lesbian dating and courtship would be a fruitful place to begin the study of lesbian relationship initiation. In the present research, the four issues raised above were investigated, including: (a) what courtship scripts lesbians used and preferred; (b) how lesbians defined dating, including what was unique about it; (c) how romantic relations were distinguished from friendship, including how they are solicited and progress; and (d) the extent to which lesbians adopted gender roles and how previous dating experience affected roles.

Developmental Issues

Whether courtship among lesbians is affected by adult development remains an open question. On the one hand, courtship scripts might be quite robust and show little variation over the life span. For example, scripts for a first date among both young heterosexual adults in their 20s and lesbians and gay men in their 20s and 30s were found to be quite similar, suggesting that compliance with cultural norms occurs across age and is particularly likely at the early stage of a relationship (Klinkenberg & Rose, 1994; Rose & Frieze, 1989; 1993).

In contrast, the little information we have about lesbians' adult development suggests that notions of dating and courtship may be affected by age. Key developmental tasks for adolescent and young adult lesbians include coming out and establishing an intimate relationship (Savin-Williams, 1995). Rose (1996) has suggested that lesbians entering their first relationship may be particularly likely to adopt a friendship script because cultural scripts for same-sex romance are not widely available. Thus, a same-sex attraction initially may be labeled or encoded as friendship rather than attraction. In young adulthood, lesbians also may lack opportunities to learn or apply other scripts due to confusion about their sexual identity, lack of role models, lack of same-age partners, or fear of anti-lesbian violence from peers (Savin-Williams, 1995). Even so, many lesbians establish their first serious relationship in their 20s.

Research on adult (30-39 years) and midlife (40-65) lesbians largely has been aimed at understanding couple relationships rather than courtship. This research emphasis reflects the heterosexist linearity of life span and relationship research, which assumes that young adult courtship will be followed by lifelong monogamy. Although often not true for heterosexuals today, this linearity may be even less applicable to lesbians for several reasons. First, although many lesbians aspire to the cultural norm of establishing a lifelong monogamous relationship with a partner, few achieve this during their early adulthood, as is prescribed by traditional values. Instead, there is a strong likelihood that lesbians may have several episodes of same-sex dating, courtship, and partnership in their lifetimes. Available research indicates that a majority of lesbians in their thirties have had at least one previous lesbian relationship (Bryant & Demian, 1990). At midlife, most lesbians in committed partnerships have had more than one previous significant relationship and a substantial proportion (33 to 43 percent) are single (Bradford & Ryan, 1991; Hall & Gregory, 1991; Sang, 1991). Second, not all lesbians endorse the concept of lifelong monogamy. West (1996) has contended that a substantial proportion of lesbians–about one in five–practice polyfidelity, that is, they are openly romantically and/or sensually involved with more than one woman concurrently. Thus, we expected to find that many lesbians would be actively dating and courting well beyond their 20s.

By midlife (40-65), it is possible to speculate based on limited information that developmental changes in dating and courtship might occur in a few areas. Lesbians between the ages of 40 and 60 have a strong sense of self as a consequence of establishing an identity separate from others and proving themselves as independent persons during their early adulthood (Kimmel & Sang, 1995). Subsequently, they may adhere less to gender roles. Because most lesbians work from economic necessity, work continues to be a strong part of their identity. However, lesbians persist in deeply valuing relationships all their lives, often wanting more time at midlife to enjoy partners, friends, and personal interests. Lesbian couples often follow a "best friend" model in their relationships that promotes equality (Rose & Roades, 1987). Friends play a particularly strong role in the lives of both coupled and single lesbians. Lesbian friends around the same age, often including ex-lovers, constitute one of the greatest sources of support for a majority of midlife lesbians (Bradford & Ryan, 1991). In addition, for at least some midlife lesbians, the idea that they would live "forever after" with one partner has been tempered by their experience (Hall & Gregory, 1991). Thus, midlife lesbians may approach dating and courtship with more maturity. For instance, they may have used more courtship scripts, developed clearer preferences for how and what kind of relationship they wish to establish, be more skilled at interpreting or signaling romantic interest, and be less affected by gender expectations.

The pattern of adult development is affected further by social age norms, historical effects, and idiosyncratic transitions (Kimmel & Sang, 1995). Lesbians who enter their first courtship today face an immensely improved social climate compared to those who came out decades ago. How these different experiences interact with age to affect dating and courtship remains to be determined.

Overall, the multiplicity of influences on dating and courtship for lesbians across the life span makes developmental changes difficult to predict. Not enough groundwork has yet been laid in terms of lesbian adult development or cohort effects to anticipate reliably how dating might be affected. Thus, our intent in the present research was to investigate how and why lesbians date, without specifically focusing on developmental issues. However, a qualitative post hoc analysis of lesbian dating was undertaken to determine whether developmental changes could be identified. To that end, responses from 38 lesbians we interviewed were examined as a function of three age groups, including young adults (20-29), adults (30-39), and midlife (40-65).

In summary, the research on lesbian dating and courtship presented here was intended to provide an exploratory descriptive analysis of lesbian relationship formation. Intensive interviews were conducted with lesbians to obtain the answer to 12 questions addressing the following themes: what courtship scripts were used, how dating was defined, how romantic relationships versus friendships were solicited and developed, and what impact gender roles and previous experience had on dating. The impact of adult development on dating and courtship for lesbians at three stages of life also was examined.

METHOD

Participants

The sample consisted of 38 lesbians between the ages of 22 to 63 years ($M = 35.9$, $SD = 10.5$). All participants were recruited at lesbian and gay community events or through friendship networks in a large midwestern city. The group studied was mostly white and middle class as determined by education and income. Ninety-two percent were white and 8% were African-American. The mean educational level of the participants was 17 years with a range of 12 to 21 years. The average income of participants was $22,687 with a range of $5,000 to $58,000. Most lesbians (89%) currently were involved in a committed relationship with another woman.

The age groups represented by participants included young adults (20-29 years; $N = 13$), adults (30-39 years; $N = 12$), and midlife adults (40-65 years; $N = 13$). The education and income of the sample are reported by age group in Table 1. Mean scores for the following variables also are included in Table 1: number of years as a lesbian, number and length of previous romantic relationships, length of current relationship, and amount of lesbian and heterosexual dating expe-

TABLE 1. Characteristics of Lesbian Participants by Age Group

	Age Group								
	Young Adulthood (20-29 yrs.) (N = 13)			Early Midlife (30-39 yrs.) (N = 12)			Later Midlife (40-65 yrs.) (N = 12)		
Characteristic	%	M	SD	%	M	SD	%	M	SD
Race									
White	100			75			100		
African-American	0			25			0		
Relationship Status									
Single	15			8			8		
Coupled	85			92			92		
Relationship Length		1.9	(2.2)		4.8	(4.2)		5.4	(4.3)
Education		17.0	(1.4)		16.7	(1.3)		6.2	(2.5)
Income		14K	(9K)		24K	(12K)		27K	(14K)[a]
Years as a lesbian		8.1	(5.2)		16.3	(3.9)		14.8	(7.2)[b]
Number previous relationships		3.5	(2.6)		4.8	(2.1)		3.6	(2.4)
Length of Previous Relationships (yrs.)		1.8	(2.4)		3.1	(2.9)		4.6	(3.6)
Dating Experience[c]									
Lesbian		2.8	(1.2)		3.2	(1.1)		3.2	(1.3)
Heterosexual		2.8	(1.1)		2.4	(0.8)		3.3	(1.2)

[a]Adult and midlife groups earned significantly more, $F_{(2,27)} = 4.36$, $p < .03$.
[b]Adult and midlife groups had been lesbians significantly longer, $F_{(2,27)} = 4.44$, $p < .03$.
[c]Adult and midlife groups had significantly longer previous relationship than younger adults $F_{(2,35)} = 3.09$, $p < .06$.
[d]5 point scale, 5 = extensive experience

rience. Analyses of variance indicated that adult and midlife lesbians earned significantly more than young lesbians and had embraced a lesbian identity longer. Mean length of romantic relationships (excluding current relationship) also was significantly longer for adult and midlife lesbians than young adults.

Measures

An interview consisting of 12 open-ended questions was administered to all participants. Age, race, income and other demographic information also was obtained. In addition, participants were asked to evaluate the extent of their lesbian and heterosexual dating experiences on a five-point scale ranging from 1 = no experience to 5 = extensive experience. Last, participants rated the frequency with which they engaged in eight gender role behaviors (e.g., asks for date, pays for activities) found by Rose and Frieze (1989) to be highly stereotyped on first dates for heterosexuals (5-point scale, 5 = occurs frequently).

Procedure

The second author interviewed all participants in their homes. Interviews took approximately 15 minutes to three hours to complete; median interview length was 45 minutes. All interviews were tape recorded and transcribed.

Coding

A coding system consisting of 48 categories was used to classify responses to the 12 open-ended questions. The categories were generated from a content analysis of the transcripts. Individual statements then were coded as belonging to specific categories. The reliability of assignment of statements to a coding category was 83%; this percentage represents the frequency of agreement between two raters who independently scored 25% of the transcripts.

RESULTS AND DISCUSSION

Courtship Experience and Scripts

Participants had considerable courtship experience. As shown in Table 1, on average, lesbians had 3 to 4.6 previous romantic relationships, in addition to their current relationship. Thus, most had from 4 to 6 relationships as a basis for describing their courtship script usage. The use of courtship scripts was assessed by reviewing each transcript to determine whether respondents had ever engaged in the romance, friendship, or sexually explicit script. About 29% of participants had used all three scripts, 47% had used two, and 29% had used only one.

As predicted, the results indicated that the friendship script was the most widely used. About 74% of lesbians reported having been friends with a woman, on at least one occasion, before becoming romantically involved with her. In comparison, 55% had used the romance script and 63% had engaged in a sexually explicit script. An example of each script taken from participant transcripts is presented in Table 2. Script preference followed a slightly different pattern, however, with half of the lesbians preferring the friendship script and half preferring the romance script across all age groups. None of the participants indicated a preference for the sexually explicit script, despite the prevalence of its use.

The most used script, friendship, generally proceeded according to the following schema. A friendship was established between two women who highly valued the emotional intimacy of their connection.

TABLE 2. Examples of Courtship Scripts Classified as Friendship, Romance, or Sexually Explicit

---

Friendship Script

We had known each other for nine years in total, and we've been a couple for almost seven of those years. We had a really strong foundation as friends. We drank together and went to the movies together. It made some foundation for a relationship. There was not that intense physical part that came all at once. I was interested in her and she had been interested in me, but neither one of us knew about the other's lesbianism. (A 25-year-old lesbian)

Romance Script

We started out dating. It wasn't like we had been friends first. After we saw each other for a few times, she said she wanted to be more than friends. Then she was expecting me to spend more time with her. It was difficult because I had four kids, school, and work, but we found that time. I started to feel like [we were] a couple after about a month. It kind of reminds me of the old joke, "Friday night you go out, Monday, you're married, and Tuesday, you make the appointment with the therapist." (A 42-year-old lesbian)

Sexually Explicit Script

I was out of town at the time. It was at a low point in my first relationship and I went traveling for a little while to San Francisco with my gay buddy. We went to a bar and there was a woman coming on to me and my friend said, "Go for it." I thought, "OK, since you are insisting." We had a great time. We essentially had a long weekend. After that, I wasn't interested. (A 51-year-old lesbian)

The intimacy and companionship of the friendship gradually led the women to a deep emotional commitment that was expressed physically, as well. The motive for establishing a friendship before getting romantically involved varied. For some, a friendship was developed first because one (or both) was unaware of her lesbianism. In other cases, the women were aware of their sexual attraction but were constrained from acting on it because one was in a serious relationship with someone else.

Although the friendship script had been used by a majority of lesbians (72%), the finding that it was preferred by fewer (50%) suggests this script may have some drawbacks. One disadvantage that was mentioned by a number of lesbians was the script's ambiguity. As one participant (age 33) explained:

> The thing that really gets cloudy in lesbian relationships for me is that I tend to fall in love with best friends–a person you would be able to confide in or go to dinner with or share secrets with or just to share a good time with. And if I'm close enough to that person, I'm going to find a love relationship and be attracted. That's where it gets real cloudy. Once I embraced a lesbian identity, it seems the people that I am best friends with wind up becoming a partner.

Even so, those who preferred the friendship script frequently did so because they believed it led to a more secure basis for a permanent commitment.

The romance script, the preferred courtship script of half of participants, had two major characteristics, including an emotional intensity and a conscious sexual attraction between the two women. The pair often began by dating or flirting with each other and, occasionally, by being fixed up on a blind date by a friend. The development of an intimate friendship, often forged by long hours on the telephone or many lengthy one-on-one conversations, combined with a strong physical attraction, quickly led to overt sexual contact. Being sexual, in turn, enhanced the couple's emotional bond. For many, becoming sexual also served as a "marker" that signified they were a couple.

One reason given for preferring the romance script was participants' emotional and physical enjoyment of the seduction. The seduction was seen as being both playful and exciting. As one lesbian (age 35) described it:

I am the one who made the first physical move in my current relationship, and that usually is not the case. But [one night] she had this lounging appearance, with her arms up behind her head, in a kind of daring position, like, "Come over here and kiss me. I dare you." There was a playful energy between us as to which one of us was going to make the first move. So, she had kind of set the stage for it, and it was up to me to go ahead with it or not. So I did. It was fun!

A second reason given for preferring a romance script was that some individuals made a clear distinction between sexual attraction and friendship and tended not to be sexually attracted to their friends. However, some of those who rejected the romance script specifically mentioned feeling uncomfortable with sexual play and seduction.

Responses classified as fitting the sexually explicit script strongly emphasized physical attraction over other aspects of the interaction. Of the 63% of respondents who had engaged in this script at least once, most had initiated the relationship at bars (46%), followed by parties (13%), ads in lesbian/gay newspapers (8%), work settings (4%), and public places (4%). A typical script involved two women meeting, being aware of a mutual sexual attraction, acting on it, and either parting ways immediately or after a relationship of relatively short duration (e.g., a few weeks or months). For instance, one woman (age 25) indicated, "On three different occasions, I went into a bar, got to know a few people there, had drinks with a woman, and went home with her. It was very casual. Just a convenient couple of weeks resulted. No long-term relationship."

Evaluations of the sexually explicit script by participants were mixed. Some felt it had been a negative experience. "It was obviously lust at first sight," a 30-year-old lesbian explained. "Before I knew it, we had gotten involved and we hadn't established any kind of friendship. That was a disaster. We had a relationship for a few turbulent months." However, positive outcomes, including the development of a friendship or romantic relationship, were cited by 58% of participants who had used this script, for example:

I was at a conference. I was involved in a lot of grassroots organizations in various cities and she is someone I met at a conference. She had come in late, and there wasn't any room for her with the party she was staying with. I said, "We can fix this."

We went home and didn't sleep all night. I heard from her several times after that. It then became more of a friendship. We lost touch after about 10 years. (a 36-year-old)

In summary, most young adult, adult, and midlife lesbians had participated in several successful courtships. A majority had used the friendship script at least once, but many also used the romance and sexually explicit scripts. However, lesbians were split about equally in their preference for friendship versus romance scripts, whereas the sexually explicit script was not endorsed by anyone as a preferred script. These results show that lesbians are versatile in their use of courtship scripts and, as expected, that issues concerning courtship are salient to lesbians throughout the life span.

Lesbian Dating and Uniqueness

Questions about whether lesbian dating existed and what was unique about it were asked to determine how much lesbians conformed to traditional views of dating. Three responses to the question of whether lesbian dating existed were obtained. Those who replied "yes," indicating they had dated in the past, were in the majority (63%). They defined dating as being a way to get to know another woman and have a good time or to explore the romantic or sexual potential of the relationship without any specific commitment in mind. This definition parallels the modern one of (heterosexual) dating as involving informal, unchaperoned, male-female interaction with no specific commitment (Murstein, 1974). One lesbian (age 23) described dating as "like what the traditional American teenager considers a date. . . . I've had women call me up and say 'Would you like to go to the movies? I'll pick you up.' And they bring flowers and all that jazz." Dating was described variously as providing a chance "to go out and see what it is all about before you hop into bed or move in with somebody," "to get to know someone before you have them in your apartment," and "to pursue an interest in another woman in a social context." One woman (age 23) offered the advice, "I agree with a gay man friend of mine who says, 'The first two months that you go out with somebody, you shouldn't have any real deep conversations. You should just have fun.'"

The second most common response to the question of whether lesbian dating exists, endorsed by 24% of participants, was to assert that courting, rather than dating, was the correct term to use. Midlife lesbians comprised the majority of participants in this group. Courting implied a more serious purpose than dating; establishing a permanent partnership was the goal. For instance, one 46-year-old woman indicated, "I prefer [the term] 'courting.' 'Dating' is not a courting process. In my experience, courting has always been [for the purpose of] getting to know the person for a potential lifetime commitment." Another lesbian (age 60) said, "Yes, dating exists [among lesbians], but minimally. . . . Unlike heterosexuals, lesbians get seriously involved more immediately instead of having a trial or dating experience. That's been my experience." "There is dating, but it is difficult dating," explained another (age 41). "We [older lesbians] tend to get very territorial, and I think that's because there are so few of us. We're like the dinosaurs–a dying breed."

The remaining 13% of participants, distributed about equally across age groups, said they had never dated and believed that dating did not exist among lesbians. These women had established all their romantic relationships via a friendship. "I never felt I was dating," indicated one lesbian (age 45). "I felt that I was going out with a friend and that we were building something greater than friendship." "I don't know if I've ever dated," claimed another (age 29). "For me, it has been kind of a mutual discovery process." Similarly, one (age 36) explained, "It has always been more knowing someone and at some point becoming attracted to them and moving from there. The period of dating isn't there."

The diversity of definitions provided above suggest that cultural norms based on heterosexual dating enjoyed limited acceptance among the lesbians we interviewed. Responses to the question, "What is unique about lesbian dating?" provided further evidence that lesbian dating did not conform to a heterosexual model. Only 23% to 31% reported that there was nothing unique about lesbian dating. (See Table 3.) The remaining participants cited four major categories of uniqueness, including freedom from gender roles, heightened intimacy/friendship, the rapid pace of lesbian relationship development, and the effects of prejudice. A fifth category, other, was used to classify miscellaneous responses mentioned only once.

The characteristics "freedom from gender roles" and "heightened intimacy" suggest that lesbian dating is more egalitarian than heterosexual dating. Behaviors usually associated with the masculine role,

TABLE 3. Descriptions of What Is Unique About Lesbian Dating by Category of Response and Age Group

Category of Response	Examples	Percentage Responding by Age Group[a]		
		Young Adult (N = 13)	Adult (N = 12)	Midlife (N = 13)
Not anything unique	It [lesbian dating] follows the heterosexual model. Someone has to adopt the male role.	31	33	23
Freedom from gender roles	One person is not in control; the roles are less defined. It's not clear who initiates.	38	25	38
Heightened intimacy/ friendship	The friendship develops as well as the sexual part. I'm more comfortable with women; I can be myself.	23	17	15
Rapid pace of relationship	Women are just ready to move in. A date could last for days and be a really intense experience.	15	0	54[b]
Effects of prejudice	There are limits on where you can go and what you can do. The need to conceal or explain the relationship	7	25	31
Other	You can lose the friendship if being lovers doesn't work out. It's hard to know if it [the date] is a friend thing or a date thing.	15	8	7

[a]Columns do not add to 100% due to multiple responses.
[b]Midlife lesbians differ significantly from other two age groups, $X^2(2) = 9.99, p < .01$.

such as who initiates and pays, were usually shared. The interaction also appeared to be less geared toward trying to impress the other person by spending money, doing courtly behaviors such as opening doors, or worrying about appearance, and more towards genuinely getting to know each other. Participants also pointed out that societal prejudice against lesbians placed limits on how openly they could date.

Significantly more midlife lesbians (54%) cited the rapid pace of relationship development as a distinctive feature of lesbian dating compared to the young adult (15%) or adult group (0), χ^2 (2) = 9.99, $p <$ .01. As one woman (age 41) explained, "the shortness of it [is unique]. You immediately find yourself in a lot more serious relationship than what you might want." Another (age 46) elaborated, "[Lesbians] get involved really quickly and then think of themselves as being in a relationship and not dating anymore. That means they live together; they're in a partnership." There are at least two possible explanations for the finding that midlife lesbians view the rapid pacing of relationships as unique. First, due to age and experience, midlife lesbians may have different values and expectations for relationships. For instance, they may be more clear about what they are looking for in a partner or be less willing to spend time in casual interactions than younger lesbians. Subsequently, they may go out with someone only if they feel there is a strong possibility for the relationship to develop. This interpretation is partially supported by findings described earlier showing that many midlife lesbians favor the term "courtship" over "dating," to signify that their goal was to establish a long-term relationship. Alternatively, midlife lesbians may have fewer available partners from which to choose. If so, the resulting anxiety about finding a companion among those who desire one may cause them to escalate the course of the relationship. Two midlife lesbians supported this interpretation by contending that it was extremely rare to find a single lesbian in the 40 to 65 age group and that, if they found one, they would feel considerable pressure to pursue her. However, more research would be required to accurately explain why midlife lesbians saw the rapid pacing of lesbian relationships as unique more so than younger ones.

In summary, dating was viewed as an informal interaction with no goal of commitment across all age groups by a majority of lesbians, most of whom had dated. However, "courtship" and "friendship" were two alternatives to dating that were preferred by some. Lesbian dating was described as being relatively free from gender roles, intimate, and quick to develop. Constraints on dating due to societal prejudice against lesbians also were noted. Midlife lesbians differed from younger lesbians in two important areas: (a) they were more likely to be seeking a serious commitment when dating or courting, and (b) they were more likely to view lesbian relationships as proceeding at a fast pace. These findings indicate that midlife lesbians may approach dating and courtship with different expectations.

Friendship versus Romance

Three questions were asked in the present research to explore how romantic relationships develop between lesbians: (a) What distinguishes a friendship from a romantic relationship? (b) What signifies to you that a change in relationship status [to being a couple] has occurred? (c) How do you let a woman know that you are interested in her romantically or know she is interested in you?

Confusion about whether a friendly versus a romantic interest motivates interactions between lesbians is a common phenomenon. One challenge for lesbians is to interpret whether friendly interest has the potential to develop into sexual attraction or is consciously or unconsciously motivated by it. In terms of distinguishing a friendship from a romance, five lesbians (13%) maintained that there was no distinction between the two. They only became partners with friends and saw the sexual aspects of the relationship as being an extension of a deep emotional commitment to the friendship. A majority (87%), however, used two main characteristics to discriminate between friendship and romance. Of these, 58 percent described friendships as being both less emotionally intense (for example, "don't invest as much emotional energy," "less tension," "talk about surface things") and lacking in sexual energy or contact. Participants also indicated being more direct about their intentions (25%) and more relaxed with friends (21%) than with potential lovers.

Lesbians may find it difficult to discern if or when a friendship has moved "over the line" into a romance. They also must create their own "markers" for transitions in their relationships due to lack of access to public rituals of commitment such as engagement and marriage. A majority of the lesbians we interviewed (68%) regarded the presence of sexual energy or contact as marking a change in status from friendship to romance. Sexual desire or behavior signaled that the relationship had become "more than friendship." Other indicators of a change in status that were commonly cited included: increased emotional closeness (40%), verbal declarations of love or commitment (37%), and living together or buying a house together (29%). On average, it took six months for this change to occur, with a range of two weeks to two years. Markers varied for many depending on the relationship, for example:

> It's been different with everybody. I've gone from knowing it's leading that way because we became more serious and gradually spent more time together–to waking up one morning and finding that all her clothes were there and she had moved in. With one woman, I realized we were a couple when every plant that she owned was in my house. I woke up one morning and had a house full of green stuff and her. I thought, "Oh, wow, I guess she's gonna stay." (a 41-year-old)

Lastly, how lesbians convey and interpret sexual attraction is an interesting question, given neither woman is likely to have been socialized to assume the initiator role. One current stereotype about lesbians is that they approach dating and courtship passively, like sheep; that is, they wait to be asked out and to be pursued sexually (Rose et al., 1993). Based on this stereotype, we predicted that lesbians would tend not to favor a direct verbal approach. This prediction was supported for two categories of behavior, including "asking for a date," and "waiting to be asked for a date." Relatively few lesbians indicated they had directly asked another woman for a date. (See Table 4.) In addition, 50% indicated on the gender role measure that they "always" or "almost always" waited to be asked for a date.

TABLE 4. Percentage of Participants (*N* = 38) Citing Behaviors that Convey Attraction

Behavior	Definition	Percentage Citing	
		Used by Self	Used by Partner
Ask for a date	Invite to an activity	18	16
Direct statements	Verbal declaration of interest	79	74
Nonverbal cues	Touching, smiling, eye contact	45	66
Attentiveness	Sexual energy, listening to partner, intuition	40	42
Indirect	Draw attention to self indirectly	18	13
Nothing	No behavioral displays	3	8

However, contrary to expectation, a majority of lesbians used direct verbal declarations to convey and read romantic interest (e.g., "tell her how I feel," "proposition her sexually," and "declare my affection"). This suggests that lesbians are far from shy in terms of signaling attraction. The second most frequently cited category of sexual signaling was the use of nonverbal proceptive behaviors. As expected, lesbians relied heavily on the nuances of touching, smiling, and maintaining eye contact to convey interest, behaviors that were described in elegant detail by many participants. The finding in Table 4 that more lesbians depended on nonverbal signals to decipher interest than they did to signal interest might imply for some a reticence to assume an active role. Alternatively, it may indicate simply that more lesbians are aware of the other woman's behavior than their own in a romantic situation. Attentiveness to the partner was the third most often mentioned means of signaling attraction. Attentiveness was defined as actively giving their attention by listening or being attuned to the needs of their prospective partners. Indirect means of attracting a partner, such as "showing off" or "telling a mutual friend," were cited by only a small percentage. An even smaller number insisted that they engaged in no behavioral displays of interest.

One age difference was observed for the measure "ask for a date." Significantly more young adult lesbians than adult or midlife lesbians said they always or almost always waited to be asked for a date, $\chi^2 (2) = 11.7$, $p < .005$. Conversely, older lesbians were more likely to have asked someone for a date. It is reasonable to speculate that, as lesbians age, they may move farther away from the traditional feminine role, or they may become comfortable adopting either role depending on the occasion.

These findings challenge the stereotype of lesbians as being passive when it comes to approaching another woman. Many participants were quite sophisticated about the process of seduction. One lesbian (age 38) described her sexual signaling system as follows:

> [If I wanted to show a woman I was interested], I would let her know by letting my sexual energy be felt–to let it flow. [That means] I would be relaxed around her and be more myself, which means that she is going to feel a sense of my sexuality, as opposed to being around someone straight or a friend. I would be perceptive about her nonverbal language. She may make slight innuendoes. I can tell if she's interested by the way she waits for

my responses to the cues that she gives me. She may lean forward when I am talking as opposed to looking off to the side. A lot of eye contact. Light touching usually happens. A softness to her voice. Her voice tone may change to being a slower paced rate of speaking, maybe with a little sexy edge to it. Her voice may drop. It is definitely not a normal speaking tone. That is a sure indication of her attraction. [To convey attraction] I would use more direct types of touching. Maybe my full hand on her arm or a couple of fingers on her leg. Legs tend to be more sexual. It's hard to give a formula. It just depends on my mood, how much I like the person, her style as it meshes with mine. It depends on so many different things.

The results concerning how romantic relationships progress suggest that lesbians have been creative in coping with the ambiguity of the friendship script, have developed markers for relationship transitions that are based primarily on sexual and emotional intimacy, and are verbally and nonverbally expressive about their attractions during courtship. Evidence that young lesbians are more tied to gender roles in terms of asking for a date than older lesbians also implies that age may be related to greater flexibility in dating.

Gender Roles and Dating Experience

A majority of lesbians (55%) either rejected gender roles by mutually negotiating their interactions or switching roles depending on the specific interaction. Others opted more consistently for a particular role either as the initiator (16%) or noninitiator (29%).

Correlational analyses were conducted on ratings of gender-role behaviors to determine if lesbians' assumption of a role paralleled that of heterosexual roles. Behaviors associated with the traditional masculine role were significantly related. How often a lesbian asked for a date was found to be positively related to how often she picked her date up (r (33) = .51, $p < .001$); planned the date (r (31) = .36, $p < .02$); did courtly behaviors during the date, such as buying flowers, giving compliments, and holding doors open (r (33) = .43, $p < .006$); paid for the date (r (33) = .34, $p < .023$); and initiated physical intimacy on the date (r (32) = .35, $p < .024$). Thus, it appeared that if a lesbian initiated a date, she also assumed other aspects of the traditional male role.

Conversely, lesbians who waited to be asked for a date were significantly unlikely to pick up the date (r (34) = $-.39, p < .05$); plan it (r (32) = $-.54, p < .01$); do courtly behaviors (r (34) = $-.36, p < .05$); or initiate physical intimacy (r (33) = $-.48, p < .01$). However, waiting to be asked for a date did *not* correlate with ratings for the item, "turned down physical intimacy," a behavior that traditionally has been assigned to heterosexual women (e.g., Peplau, Rubin, & Hill, 1977). What these findings suggest is that lesbians who assume the feminine reactive role in dating, unlike heterosexual women, do not play a restrictive role in terms of limiting sexual contact.

Previous research has demonstrated a relationship between dating experience and gender roles, with more experienced heterosexual daters engaging in more stereotypical behavior (Rose & Frieze, 1989). The impact of lesbian and heterosexual experience on ratings of the eight gender role behaviors was examined using analysis of variance to test for mean differences between inexperienced daters (i.e., those with ratings of 1 or 2 on a 5-point scale) and experienced ones (i.e., ratings of 4 or 5 on the scale). Experienced lesbian daters were found to have initiated physical intimacy on their dates ($M = 3.19$) significantly more often than those with little lesbian dating experience ($M = 1.93$), F (1,28) = 6.84, $p < .02$. Lesbian dating experience was not significantly related to other gender behaviors. Those with extensive heterosexual dating experience were found to reject physical intimacy more often ($M = 2.66$) than those with little experience ($M = 1.83$), F (1,30) = 5.83, $p < .02$; no other effects were found.

Last, the relationship between age and the "initiate physical intimacy" measure was explored. Adult and midlife lesbians were found to be significantly more likely to have initiated sexual behavior ($M = 3.00$ and 2.87, respectively) than young adult lesbians ($M = 1.82$), F (2,32) = 3.24, $p < .05$.

In sum, the findings concerning gender roles and dating experience suggest that lesbian dating experience enables women to freely initiate sexual interactions, whereas heterosexual dating experience reinforces the role of the woman as the sexual "limit setter." Thus, it appears that the use of gender roles as practiced by lesbians does not dictate sexual interactions. Also, as lesbians get older and have more lesbian dating experience, they appear to become more comfortable with initiating sexual intimacy.

Age and Courtship

Research on adult development and romantic relationships has not yet been undertaken with a lesbian life cycle as the norm. For example, courtship has been rooted in the developmental phase of young heterosexual adulthood by most relationship researchers and developmental psychologists. Most lesbians do not follow this model. Thus, only a few tentative predictions concerning courtship and age were advanced. Specifically, midlife lesbians were expected to be less bound by gender roles, to be more mature in terms of how they approached courtship, as expressed in terms of having more realistic expectations and being aware of their own needs, and to be more skilled at communicating or interpreting interpersonal attraction.

The four significant results reported earlier provide support for the general direction of our predictions; that is, midlife lesbians undertake courtship with greater freedom from gender roles and with more maturity. Midlife lesbians were found to differ significantly from young adults in terms of having been a lesbian longer, perceiving lesbian dating as having the serious goal of commitment, describing lesbian relationships as developing at a rapid pace, and to be more likely to ask for a date and to initiate physical intimacy. Based on our review of each transcript as a whole, we labeled the midlife lesbians as being more "purposive" in their attitudes and behaviors than the young adult or adult group. Midlife lesbians often spoke specifically to the issue of having approached relationships more casually in their youth or having been motivated by physical attraction, sexual gratification, or other needs unrelated to what they considered now to be more important. As they aged, they became more concerned about the "attachment-worthiness" of a partner; that is, whether the necessary warmth, respect, and reciprocal liking necessary to sustain a relationship was present before pursuing a sexual relationship. Once they judged these attributes to be present, they acted quickly. Thus, their current behaviors seemed to be motivated by a more accurate assessment of their needs and greater experience concerning what will sustain a relationship.

Midlife lesbians also spoke to other changes over the course of their lifetime that affected courtship. Many mentioned enjoying no longer having to conform to the butch-femme roles that dominated the bar scene in their youth. They also appreciated the relatively greater freedom they felt to be openly lesbian and being able to find partners outside the bars due to the growth of the lesbian community.

CONCLUSIONS

Courtship was found to be highly relevant to lesbians throughout the life span. Most had established several long-term relationships and utilized a variety of courtship scripts. The friendship and romance scripts were most preferred, with the sexually explicit script having been widely practiced but not preferred. These results suggest that lesbians prefer courtship and relationships that emphasize emotional intimacy either more so or equally with sexual desire, as opposed to favoring sexual attraction over intimacy. Both increasing intimacy and sexuality were used to mark when a relationship was "going beyond" friendship. Contrary to the stereotype of lesbians as being passive in approaching partners, most were found to be quite direct in their verbal expressions of affection, as well as very skilled in the use of proceptive nonverbal cues to signal attraction.

Definitions of lesbian dating and uniqueness, as well as the findings concerning gender roles, illustrated that lesbians either rejected or modified contemporary heterosexual practices. Freedom from gender roles contributed to an egalitarian approach to dating that may have enhanced the intimacy and rapid pacing regarded as unique to lesbian courtship. Most lesbians did not adopt active versus reactive roles in dating. However, those who did rejected heterosexual notions of the woman as the sexual limit-setter. Age and lesbian dating experience also were found to be related to initiating sexual intimacy. These findings imply that even when lesbians conform to some aspects of heterosexual roles, they do not necessarily reproduce heterosexual power relations in terms of sexual behavior. Furthermore, their court-ships may be more sexually satisfying, because satisfaction with sex has been shown to be linked to equality in initiating and refusing sex (Blumstein & Schwartz, 1983).

Courtship among older lesbians was found to differ from younger ones both as a function of maturity and historical change, with midlife lesbians being more oriented toward establishing an emotional commit-ment, being less tied to gender roles, and expressing appreciation for greater societal tolerance of lesbians. However, conclusions concerning adult development were limited by the small sample size and narrow scope of questions investigated. In addition, the relatively few age differences that were observed suggest that courtship is a strong script in the sense that it is highly codified by cultural norms and may not change much with age. Nevertheless, the results suggest that one interesting area for future research might focus specifically on retrospective evaluations of how courtship has changed over the life course.

Clinical Implications

The findings from the present study have implications for therapists who have lesbian clients. Understanding oneself in relation to others is central to the therapeutic process. Information regarding how lesbians from different age groups negotiate dating and courtship can facilitate this process for clients. Although our sample was limited in size, certain guidelines for therapists can be derived from the data which are consistent with five of the tenets of a feminist theory of psychological practice (Brabeck & Brown, 1997).

Remaining close to the "data of experience." Any theory of lesbian relationship development must remain close to lesbians' real-life experiences–it should be "sappho-centric." Throughout the interview process, participants discussed their relationship histories with candor. We sought meaning of their stories within the context of the relationships we developed with them, and it was our hope to give an accurate voice to their stories. We acknowledge, however, that neither their nor our understanding of relationships is static. Given a different setting or point in time, participants' stories may have varied, and we may have drawn different conclusions. We hope that therapists reading this article will learn as much from the process of our research as they do from the content, and create understanding from both the "data of experience," as well as from human connection.

Embracing diversity. Historically, little has been written about lesbians across the life span. The present research was intended to begin to close this gap in knowledge. Although the participants we interviewed were homogeneous in terms of race and class, their life experiences were quite diverse. It is likely that even more diverse stories may have been obtained using a sample that was more heterogeneous in terms of race, ethnicity, class or ability. We caution therapists to be mindful of the differences among lesbians and to embrace diversity as a foundation for their practice.

Expanding notions of identity and multiple subjectivities. Throughout the research process, we viewed the women as active participants in defining their realities. The interview process was interactive, and at no point did we view ourselves as the only or most important voice of knowledge. During the interviews, we witnessed participants derive new meanings from their relationships and give voice to experiences that previously had been unspoken. Throughout the process, we learned as much about ourselves as we did about participants. For example, based on female socialization, we anticipated that only a minority of lesbians would have participated in casual sexual encounters. Instead, we found that many women had engaged in this script, as well as reported as having learned a great deal about themselves in the process, whereas others rejected the casual sex script entirely. Thus, we recommend that clinicians acknowledge multiple subjectivities within the context of the therapeutic relationship.

Reformulating understanding psychological distress from feminist theory. Traditional psychology places the experiences of the dominant group (e.g., men, heterosexuals) at the center as "normal," "right," or "healthy." The functioning of marginalized groups (e.g., lesbians) is viewed as being deficient by comparison. In terms of relationship development specifically, contemporary heterosexual norms endorse lifelong monogamy as superior to other types of romantic pairings. If the dominant view of permanent pairings as being "better" is internalized by a lesbian client, it may be helpful for the therapist to help her explore alternative paradigms for assessing her own behavior that are based more on lesbian experience. This reformulation takes what was formerly considered to be evidence of a deficit or defect and reinterprets it as evidence of creative resistance in the face of oppression (Brabeck & Brown, 1997).

In conclusion, the findings of the current study can inform therapists' work with lesbian clients. It is our hope that therapists will benefit from both the content and process of the research presented here and will use it to foster growth in their clients.

REFERENCES

Bailey, B. L. (1998). *From front porch to back seat: Courtship in twentieth century America.* Baltimore: The Johns Hopkins University Press.

Bechdel, A. (1995). *Unnatural dykes to watch out for.* Ithaca, NY: Firebrand Books.

Blumstein, P. W., & Schwartz, P. (1983). *American couples.* New York: William Morrow.

Brabeck, M., & Brown, L. (1997). Feminist theory and psychological practice. In J. Worell & N. G. Johnson (Eds.), *Shaping the future of feminist psychology: Education, research, and practice* (pp. 15-35). American Psychological Association: Washington, DC.

Bradford, J., & Ryan, C. (1991). Who we are: Health concerns of middle-aged lesbians. In B. Sang, J. Warshow, & A. Smith (Eds.), *Lesbians at midlife: The creative transition* (pp. 147-163). San Francisco: Spinsters.

Bryant, S., & Demian (1990, May/June). *Partners: Newsletter for gay and lesbian couples* (available from Partners, Box 9685, Seattle, WA 98109).

Cate, R. M., & Lloyd, S. A. (1992). *Courtship.* Newbury Park, CA: Sage.

Cini, M. A., & Malafi, T. N. (1991, March). Paths to intimacy: Lesbian and heterosexual women's scripts of early relationship development. Paper presented at the Association for Women in Psychology conference, Hartford, CT.

DeLaria, L. (1995). Ms. DeLaria's dating tips for dykes. In C. Flowers (Ed.), *Out, loud, and laughing* (pp. 57-68). New York: Anchor.

Eisenbach, H. (1996). *Lesbianism made easy.* New York: Crown.

Gagnon, J. (1977). *Human sexualities.* Glenview, IL: Scott, Foresman.

Ginsberg, G. P. (1988). Rules, scripts and prototypes in personal relationship. In S. W. Duck (Ed.), *Handbook of personal relationships* (pp. 23-39). New York: John Wiley.

Grammick, J. (1984). Developing a lesbian identity. In T. Darty & S. Potter (Eds.), *Women identified women* (pp. 31-44). Palo Alto, CA: Mayfield.

Hall, M., & Gregory, A. (1991). Subtle balances: Love and work in lesbian relationships. In B. Sang, J. Warshow, & A. Smith (Eds.), *Lesbians at midlife: The creative transition* (pp. 122-133). San Francisco: Spinsters.

Kimmel, D. C., & Sang, B. E. (1995). Lesbians and gay men in midlife. In A. R. D'Augelli & C. J. Patterson (Eds.), *Lesbian, gay, and bisexual identities over the life span* (pp. 190-214). New York: Oxford University Press.

Klinkenberg, D., & Rose, S. (1994). Dating scripts of lesbians and gay men. *Journal of Homosexuality, 26,* 23-35.

Lapidus, J. (1995). Procrasti-dating. In K. Jay (Ed.), *Dyke life.* New York: Basic Books.

Laws, J. L., & Schwartz, P. (1977). *Sexual scripts: The social construction of female sexuality.* Washington, DC: University Press of America.

McDaniel, J. (1995). *The lesbian couple's guide.* New York: HarperCollins.

Modell, J. (1983). Dating becomes the way of American youth. In D. Levine, L. P. Moch, L. A. Tilly, J. Modell, & E. Pleck (Eds.), *Essays on the family and historical change* (pp. 169-175). College Station: Texas A & M University Press.

Moore, M. M. (1985). Nonverbal courtship patterns in women: Context and consequences. *Ethology and Sociobiology, 6,* 237-247.

Murstein, B. I. (1974). *Love, sex and marriage through the ages.* New York: Springer.

Peplau, L.A., Rubin, Z. & Hill, C.T. (1977). Sexual Intimacy in dating couples. *Journal of Social Issues, 33* (2), 86-109.

Perper, T., & Weis, D. L. (1987). Proceptive and rejective strategies of U.S. and Canadian college women. *Journal of Sex Research, 23,* 455-480.

Rose, S. (1996). Lesbian and gay love scripts. In E. D. Rothblum & L. A. Bond

(Eds.), *Preventing heterosexism and homophobia* (pp. 151-173). Newbury Park, CA: Sage.

Rose, S., & Frieze, I. H. (1989). Young singles' contemporary dating scripts. *Sex Roles, 28,* 1-11.

Rose, S., & Frieze, I. H. (1993). Young singles' scripts for a first date. *Gender and Society, 3,* 258-268.

Rose, S., & Roades, L. (1987). Feminism and women's friendships. *Psychology of Women Quarterly, 11,* 243-354.

Rose, S., Zand, D., & Cini, M. (1993). Lesbian courtship scripts. In E. D. Rothblum & K. A. Brehony (Eds.), *Boston marriages: Romantic but asexual relationships among contemporary lesbians* (pp. 70-85). Amherst: University of Massachusetts Press.

Rothblum, E. D., & Brehony, K. A. (1993). *Boston marriages: Romantic but asexual relationships among contemporary lesbians.* Amherst: University of Massachusetts Press.

Sang, B. (1991). Moving towards balance and integration. In B. Sang, J. Warshow, & A. Smith (Eds.), *Lesbians at midlife: The creative transition* (pp. 206-214). San Francisco: Spinsters.

Sausser, G. (1990). *More lesbian etiquette.* Freedom, CA: Crossing Press.

Savin-Williams, R. C. (1995). Dating and romantic relationships among gay, lesbian, and bisexual youths. In R. C. Savin-Williams and K. M. Cohen (Eds.), *The lives of lesbians, gays and bisexuals: Children to adults* (pp. 166-180). New York: Harcourt Brace.

West, C. (1996). *Lesbian polyfidelity.* San Francisco: Bootlegger Publishing.

Making Up for Lost Time: Chemically Dependent Lesbians in Later Midlife

Dana G. Finnegan
Emily B. McNally

SUMMARY. This article focuses on lesbians in later midlife who are in recovery (for at least six months) from chemical dependency and on the ways the traumatic effects of their chemical dependency affect and influence the issues they face, the decisions they make, the actions they take, and, most especially, the relationships they have with both self and others. Although earlier midlife (from 40 to 50) is an important time, we will focus on the later years (from 50 to 60) because they seem to comprise the critical decade, the time when "old selves are lost and new ones come into being" (Stein, 1983, p. 3). *[Article copies available for a fee from The Haworth Document Delivery Service: 1-800-342-9678. E-mail address: <getinfo@haworthpressinc.com> Website: <http://www.haworthpressinc.com>]*

KEYWORDS. Lesbian, midlife, chemical dependency, recovery, sexual identity, support networks, drugs/alcohol

---

Dana G. Finnegan, PhD, CAC, is a certified alcoholism counselor in private practice, specializing in the treatment of issues relating to recovery from addictions, primarily with lesbian and gay people. She is co-founder and current board member of the National Association of Lesbian and Gay Addiction Professionals. Emily B. McNally, PhD, CAC, is a licensed psychologist in private practice, specializing in the treatment of sexual identity issues and issues relating to recovery from addictions. She is co-founder and current board member of the National Association of Lesbian and Gay Addiction Professionals.

[Haworth co-indexing entry note]: "Making Up for Lost Time: Chemically Dependent Lesbians in Later Midlife." Finnegan, Dana G., and Emily B. McNally. Co-published simultaneously in *Journal of Gay & Lesbian Social Services* (Harrington Park Press, an imprint of The Haworth Press, Inc.) Vol. 11, No. 2/3, 2000, pp. 105-118; and: *Midlife Lesbian Relationships: Friends, Lovers, Children, and Parents* (ed: Marcy R. Adelman) Harrington Park Press, an imprint of The Haworth Press, Inc., 2000, pp. 105-118. Single or multiple copies of this article are available for a fee from The Haworth Document Delivery Service [1-800-342-9678, 9:00 a.m. - 5:00 p.m. (EST). E-mail address: getinfo@haworthpressinc.com].

105

INTRODUCTION

For many women, midlife (the period between ages 40 to 60) is one of the most challenging times in life and brings with it a host of issues, problems, and questions that require the exercise of ingenuity, stability, and life skills. If the person in midlife is a lesbian, then other important factors also come into play–primarily, the way she relates to her sexual orientation, the way she deals with having a stigmatized identity, and the way her being in or out of the closet affects and influences her questioning, planning, decision-making, and relationships. In addition, if the midlife lesbian is recovering from chemical dependency (CD), the traumatic effects of addiction alter her life experiences in many different and powerful ways–for example, many CD lesbians suffer from chronic depression; most have impaired cognitive and affective skills; many have problems with proper self-care; all have lost time that can never be regained; and almost all have engaged in behaviors that have far-reaching effects on their lives (Bean, 1981; Finnegan & McNally, 1996; Herman, 1992; Hull, 1987; Khantzian, 1981; Krystal, 1988; Mack, 1981; Pandina, 1982). Thus, CD lesbians belong to a special population of women whose life circumstances shape and determine their reactions to and handling of later midlife so that their experiences are different from those of other, nonchemically dependent women.

Focus of This Article

This article will focus on lesbians in midlife who are in recovery (for at least six months) from chemical dependency and on the ways the traumatic effects of their chemical dependency affect and influence the issues they face, the decisions they make, the actions they take, and, most especially, the relationships they have with both self and others. Although earlier midlife (from 40 to 50) is a time of important changes and questions about life, the later years (from 50 to 60) seem to compose the critical decade, the time when "the psyche explodes, and the lava from this eruption forms and reforms the landscapes of our psychological lives" (Stein, 1983, p. 2). As the Group for Research on Mid-life and Older Women (Bennett, 1995) states, "The majority of transitions [in older women's lives] occur in the decade from age 50 to 60" (p. 17). In their study on the significance of women's 50th birthdays to their individuation process, Niemela and

Lento (1993) note that their "50th birthdays shook these women up, starting a process of rethinking and re-evaluation of their entire lives" (p. 124).

Pearlman (1993) describes what she terms "late midlife astonishment" as

> a sudden awareness of the acceleration of aging characterized by feelings of amazement and despair at the recognition of multiple losses and changes brought about [by] or occurring simultaneously with the increase of age. (p. 2)

Stein's description (1983) vividly captures the power and the importance of this process:

> At midlife there is a crossing-over from one psychological identity to another. The self goes through a transformation. . . . [It is] a time when persons are going through a fundamental shift in their alignment with life and with the world, and this shift has psychological and religious meaning beyond the interpersonal and social dimensions. Midlife is a crisis of the spirit. In this crisis, old selves are lost and new ones come into being. (p. 3)

Although this process certainly can start earlier, the age of 50 seems to issue a wake-up call, which jolts many women into action. As a result of the far-reaching traumatic effects of their addiction, CD recovering lesbians face a particularly formidable task in later midlife, rather like being dropped into a foreign country without knowing the language and without having a map.

Recovery Issues for CD Lesbians

The majority of CD recovering lesbians entering this critical decade between 50 and 60 bring with them major disadvantages. These women have had to pour most of their energies into the profound transformational effort required to recover and stay that way. In what is often a life-or-death struggle, much if not most of their energy has been channeled into performing the most basic tasks of recovery. These are tasks such as not drinking or drugging one day (sometimes one minute) at a time, learning how to deal with the pain and rawness of life without anesthesia, forming supportive relationships with other recovering people, developing a network of people who can help them maintain recovery, and severing or trying to control relationships with those who pose a threat to their recovery (e.g., still-active addicts or homophobic, non-supportive family members).

Most of these women are not well prepared for life in recovery. Not only have they had to focus much of their time and energy on the basic tasks of recovery, but the trauma of their active chemical dependency has left many of them with varying degrees of impairment of their cognitive and emotional skills. Thus, many of these women lack the skills necessary for creating and maintaining relationships, making and keeping boundaries, communicating, identifying and asserting needs, and identifying and verbalizing feelings. In addition, most people traumatized by chemical dependency suffer from a disruption in the skills of self-care (Bean, 1981; Herman, 1992; Khantzian, 1981; Krystal, 1988; Mack, 1981), skills ranging from how to balance a budget and deal with anger and rage to how to schedule time, get proper medical treatment, and avoid inflicting self-harm. Many are plagued by other addictions (e.g., smoking, compulsive overeating, and credit abuse). Many–some research cites statistics as high as 70% (Weber, 1977) and 80% (Grice, 1994) of CD women–have been sexually abused. Many are seriously depressed and are struggling with the losses inflicted by their active addiction (e.g., money, career opportunities, and relationships). Above all, however, all CD women in recovery face the inescapable fact that they have lost years to decades of their lives to the ravages of their addiction and that they cannot get that time back.

The upshot of all these traumatic consequences is that CD *women* are more likely than non-CD women to be depressed and to struggle with many more problems and burdens when they enter midlife. *Lesbians* who are chemically dependent must deal not only with the traumatic consequences of their addiction but also with the consequences of their sexual orientation.

Issues of Lesbian Sexual Identity and Recovery

The issues engendered by a lesbian sexual identity are many and varied. Some women have known that they were lesbian long before they began their recovery; some of them have been out, others closeted. But when they enter recovery, they then need to rework their process of developing and coming to terms with their lesbian identity because, as McNally (1989) and Kus (1988) found, people in active chemical dependency cannot proceed past what is a fairly adolescent-like stage of identity development. This stage involves such attitudes and behaviors as dividing the world into them and us, immersing themselves in a lesbian world (whether of actual people or books) and thus isolating from the larger culture, and/or drowning themselves in a drinking culture. As one recovering lesbian in McNally's study (1989) said,

> It's important for me to remember how accepted, how normal it was to not only drink, but to get drunk, and how much my lesbian identity and social life and structuring, and everything had to do with alcohol. (p. 141)

This reworking involves profound changes in values, behaviors, and companions–changes that tend to seriously affect the relationships lesbians have in recovery. In order to maintain their recovery, these women must begin to address and deal with their internalized homophobia and the pressures of their stigmatized identity so that the self-hatred they have medicated with alcohol/drugs will ease and become less threatening. Frequently, these recovering women must sever or radically alter their relationships with other lesbians who were their friends, companions, and lovers during their active addiction because many of these women still may be addicted. To continue to socialize with them constitutes a great danger to the CD lesbians' recovery. They must find or establish new support networks such as Alcoholics Anonymous (AA). Depending on their degree of "outness," they may attend gay/lesbian meetings or "straight" meetings. Or they may seek out other women's groups to get support. They must, in effect, find new ways and a new social/emotional milieu in order to develop and maintain their identity as lesbians who are in recovery from chemical dependency.

Other women may be in recovery for long periods of time and not realize that they might be lesbians. Although they may have had some sense that they were attracted to women, their active addiction helped them block off their awareness and remain in denial about their sexual identity. When they get into recovery, that denial may continue for a long time. However, as the recovery process proceeds, these women's cognitive and emotional skills begin to clear and start to operate more effectively. Thus, in recovery they get the opportunity to consider the possibility that they are lesbians. In effect, they get to open their eyes and ears to their thoughts and feelings about possibly loving other women.

Although these new possibilities can be both challenging and exciting, they also may feel threatening as recovering women start coming to terms with the consequences of their new and different sexual identities. These women often must radically alter relationships with husbands or boyfriends, deal with the reactions of children and other family members, face the sometimes negative responses of straight AA members who have been a part of their recovery, and learn how to be lesbians–how to socialize as lesbians, and how to be sexual with women, and how to relate to other lesbians, themselves, and the outer world.

Recovery from chemical dependency provides lesbians with the opportunity and the challenge to transform their lives, but such processes make people vulnerable and demand many skills and strengths. For example, creating a new life free of alcohol/drugs and separate from people who are still involved in a drugging world demands courage, self-determination, perseverance, and creativity. The process of transformation when coupled with the issues, problems, questions, and tasks of later midlife constitutes a formidable task, a juggling act of major proportions and far-reaching implications since the later midlife decade raises all kinds of concerns. Some concerns are new, but many are familiar concerns that have taken on new meanings and import in these years–for example, career paths; retirement; relationships to aging (and perhaps ill) parents; relationships to children, stepchildren, grandchildren, nephews, and nieces; love relationships; friendships; health problems; physical aging; and existential questions such as "Who am I?" "What does my life mean?" and "What is my spiritual path?"

The collision between these midlife concerns and lesbians' recovery processes is very powerful and can shake women's faith in themselves and their relationship both to the world and to those in their world. As women proceed in their recovery, they begin to get free of the obscuring effects of alcohol and/or drugs and are able to see their lives more clearly, sometimes for the first time. It is as if they are waking from a long sleep and are viewing a world that is foreign to them. They become aware of values and beliefs, of wants and wishes they may have long suppressed. This kind of awakening, when coupled with the sometimes-insistent questions raised by later midlife, challenges whatever secure feelings women may have gained from the routine of their earlier lives. For example, some women drank/ drugged in order to stay in heterosexual marriages so that they could feel "normal." Once they enter recovery they may begin to question whether this is what they want. This questioning may then be intensified by concerns of later midlife such as a strong sense of time passing, or of life not having the meaning they want it to have. To have long-held beliefs and values suddenly, or even slowly, called into question oftentimes shakes women's faith in themselves and the world they have always known. On the other hand, this questioning also can be an exhilarating experience of transformation, of taking on or creating new identities, and of forging new bonds with self and others.

THE WOMEN

What follows here are some examples of CD recovering lesbians' experiences as they encounter and deal with later midlife. The women described here are a composite of many women from the New York/ New Jersey metropolitan area with whom we have worked over a number of years. These are not their real names. Since this topic is so complex, it is important to note that these examples are representative of only a few of the issues that CD lesbians deal with in later midlife.

After many years of drinking alcoholically, *Nancy* finally found her way into AA and after a year and a half of relapses got sober. Three years later, at the age of 52, she just now is able to attend to anything beyond the demanding struggle to get and stay sober. During that struggle, she had to sever her ties with many of the lesbians and gay men who made up her created family because many of them continued drinking around her when she needed to be surrounded by clean and sober people. She also finally broke up with her lover of five-and-a-half years because the lover continued to drink alcoholically.

Nancy has formed a number of friendships with AA people, but the majority of them are straight because she lives in a small town where there are only two gay/lesbian meetings in the whole surrounding area. She lives alone, goes to a number of meetings, and mostly focuses on her recovery. But she is having a hard time because she is faced with issues of later midlife intertwined with and intensified by issues of recovery. She must grieve the time she has lost because of her addiction at the same time she must recognize that her life is more than half over. She must come to terms with lost career opportunities because of her addiction and with the fact that there is not a lot of time to "catch up." She also must deal with getting older and the effects of aging on both her body and her spirit, and how that relates to not having a partner with whom to share her life. She worries that she will not be able to attract a new lover, partly because she fears her aging body makes her physically unattractive. In addition, her chemical dependency has contributed to her having a distorted body image, which has shaken her self-esteem.

These fears are added to by the deficits in her cognitive, emotional, and social skills, deficits created by her addiction. For years she used alcohol to ease her social interactions, a procedure that worked for her at the time but deprived her of important learning experiences and much-needed practice of social skills. Now, when she meets a woman who interests her, she feels awkward and scared because she does not know much about how to flirt or date or even carry on a conversation that will lead anywhere. It is a strain for her to want to find a life partner, to feel as if she does not have the necessary skills to do so, and to constantly stay alert to the dangers of relapse.

Barbara, on the other hand, does not worry particularly about relapse. At age 53, she has been sober for 12 years and has built a solid identity as a recovering person. She has numerous friends in AA. But she does not have a lover and has experienced difficulty finding and forming long-term relationships. In addition, she is, in effect, an orphan–her mother died soon after Barbara got sober, her father three years later. And, then, her beloved older sister died of breast cancer a year ago.

So Barbara finds herself at loose ends so far as close relationships go. Her AA friendships are the heart of her emotional life; they have provided her with the support, love, and encouragement that have enabled her to change, grow, and move ahead in her life. Ironically, it is the support of this AA extended family that has enabled her to face head-on the challenges of her later midlife. Barbara wants to establish a new career as an occupational therapist and do work that is meaningful to her, but then she would have to move to another state to get the kind of schooling she needs and thus leave her AA family behind. In effect, she would have to take the risk of separating from her family and facing the outside world, a developmental task that usually occurs at an earlier age. In some ways, however, she is emotionally younger than her age because of the developmental damages of addiction. Thus, although career changes and longings for change are a part of this stage of later midlife, the risks are compounded for CD women.

This career change would also mean going to school with people who are, for the most part, much younger than she so that making new friends might be somewhat harder. But even though these conditions would pose various difficulties for her, she feels that she needs to make up for the years she has lost during her active addiction and that time is passing so she won't get another opportunity. Strengthened by her AA relationships and recovery process, Barbara has the confidence to take the risks and follow her dream.

Toni, at 54, is grappling with other issues. In the course of her 15 years of recovery, she has been befriended, guided, and supported by numerous people in AA, many of them gay men. During this time, she has lost her sponsor and seven other gay male friends to death from AIDS; she also has lost several other friends to lung and breast cancer. Many of the gay male friends were younger than she, and the others were uncomfortably close to her in age. At this point in her life, she is beset by huge existential questions raised not only by the crisis of later midlife but also by so many losses–What does life mean? What does *my* life mean? Is it too late in my life for me to start again? What's the use of trying to make friends, of having relationships, when they are cut short? How can I go on living in the face of such loss? These questions are made more intense by the long-term effects of addiction, including powerful suicidal feelings coupled with the knowledge of having lived on the edge of death during the active years of addiction. Toni must come to terms with issues of living and dying and must do so in the company of some people who are dying or close to death. She must struggle with feeling she has no right to talk about her suicidal feelings, her fears, in the face of others with AIDS. Coming to terms with such deep grief for the loss of beloved friends, the loss of her youth, the loss of meaning as a result of the traumas she has endured demands great courage and much hard psychological and spiritual work. But hard as these tasks are, Toni does have a support network provided by her recovery community. And she has the teachings of the AA program to help her with her spiritual struggles.

June, Esther, and *Doris* also are undergoing an existential "crisis of the spirit," questioning their relationships with Life, with Self, and with a higher power. *June,* who is 57, always wanted to go to college, but during the years-long course of her addiction never dreamed she could. Now that she is sober, her dream is a definite possibility. But to bring it about, she must struggle with later midlife fears that she is too old, that it is too late to embark on such an ambitious course of action. In addition, she must work through fears that her addiction has damaged her abilities to think and memorize. She also worries that she has lost so much time to her addiction that she can never catch up. And she is hampered in her process by not having very many role models of CD recovering lesbians going back to school much later in life. At the same time, however, the teachings of AA and the people in AA encourage her to live her life to the fullest because she came so close to losing it.

Esther, at 55, is alone and fearful of her aloneness. When she was sober for about a year, she divorced her husband and began the daunting task of coming out. Now, in the second year of her sobriety, she faces the formidable tasks of learning to maintain her sobriety while at the same time developing her fledgling lesbian identity, both of which tasks are made more difficult because she is "new at the game." At the same time, she must deal with various challenges of later midlife such as feeling that she is too old to start over (either in recovery or in her sexual orientation), feeling that her body's aging process is "betraying" her, thus causing her to doubt her desirability, and feeling that she is in the midst of a transformation which she doesn't understand fully but finds exciting. Although she has had a few brief relationships, she has not yet managed to form a long-term one and currently inhabits what Lavender calls "the relational void" (1997, p. 12). She has to contend with all her fears and doubts and sometimes feels her higher power has abandoned her; yet, at the same time, she is grateful that her recovery has provided her with the chance to get in touch with her sexual orientation and live as her "true self," and that her recovery community provides her with support for the major transformations in which she is engaged.

Unlike Esther, *Doris* has always known she was a lesbian and has lived her life according to that knowledge. She has had to wrestle with various issues as she traverses later midlife: first she had to sever many of the ties she had to women with whom she drank because they could not support her efforts to get and stay sober; then she and her lover of 19 years broke up during the time Doris was ill with Hodgkin's disease. Now, four years sober, at the age of 59, she is in remission and facing the possibility of not having another long-term relationship. She knows now that her nineteen-year relationship was based on the dynamics of addiction–she was the addict, her lover was caretaker and controller of the addict. When Doris got and stayed sober, the precarious balance that depended on the addiction tipped and finally the relationship broke apart. What troubles Doris is her realization that she does not know much about how to have a relationship when sober. To try to learn how is an awesome task at any age; it is a task made more difficult by the doubts and worries that can accompany later midlife, such as: Am I too old to change? Is there time for me to learn about and benefit from changing? Am I too old to be attractive to someone? At the same time, Doris also is struggling to activate her long dormant creative drive and realize her artistic potential as a way of coming to terms with her mortality.

Sara faces other dilemmas. In her third year of recovery, she turned 50 and started seriously questioning her life, her marriage, and her sexuality. She began to realize that she had always been drawn to other women and that while she loved her husband of 22 years, she wasn't satisfied either emotionally or sexually. She was able to carry out this later midlife task of looking at and evaluating her life because her thinking is much clearer in recovery. After much soul-searching, reading, and talking with other women, Sara realized she is a lesbian. Since then, she has immersed herself in the experience of her new self–dating lots of women, becoming active in lesbian groups, and proudly proclaiming her sexual identity. It is as though she has to make up for time lost to her addiction and to have it all before she gets any older.

Although many women come out at midlife and later midlife, CD lesbians who do so face issues specific to their recovering status. Coming out for Sara (and others like her) is a major transformative process that can generate extremely powerful feelings such as exhilaration, fear, curiosity, anger, anxiety, and excitement. Sara has to learn how to keep her emotional balance in the midst of such feelings so that she can go through this process in a way that protects her recovery. Lesbian and gay AA mentors and/or straight allies can help enormously by supporting her throughout the process and teaching her how to stay sober in the face of the ferment of change.

Mona, at 54, is also trying to make up for the time she lost to her addiction and is also facing major changes. After establishing her recovery, she has turned to face the issues presented to her. She is not out to her large family, and she is the only sibling who is not married. As such, she is the one who is expected to care for her elderly and unwell parents. She has had to juggle this task with the demands of maintaining a relationship with a woman who is focused on pursuing her own career. Now, after devoting her energies to her parents and her relationship during the last five years, Mona wants to change her life. The strength and support she has gained from her recovery coupled with the urgency of moving ahead at this critical time in her life have brought her to this place of change. She is faced with tough choices. She wants to pursue her considerable creative talent for making pottery, and she wants to do so in New Mexico, far from her parents, her family, and her lover who is not willing to leave her career and move. Mona is struggling with having to choose between leaving her family and lover on the East Coast or staying and not following her new life path. Hard as this process may be, Mona feels that if she does not "follow her bliss," her soul will shrivel up and die.

Alice, too, must struggle with difficult choices. Her younger lover had to relocate to keep her position in her company and wants Alice to come live with her in the new city. She feels that since Alice is 57 she should take early retirement and move. Aside from the difficulties presented by moving to a new and strange city, Alice must cope with the consequences of a major life decision–whether she is ready to retire, when she should do it, what it will mean in her life, and how she will handle the pressures of trying to match her retired lifestyle with her younger lover's active career life. Currently, Alice is struggling with questions of how to find the right life path for her and whether she can do these things and still maintain her sobriety.

CONCLUSION

When lesbians enter midlife, especially later midlife, they face many challenges and must make important decisions. Lesbians who are in CD recovery deal with all of these same kinds of challenges and choice making, but they do so from a different perspective. In their struggle to free themselves from their life-threatening addiction, they have come face to face with their own death and have chosen life. In recovery, they have learned that "life is not a dress rehearsal" and that they should make the most of their lives. But they have been traumatized by their addiction. They are often hampered by impaired intellectual and emotional functioning and impaired self-care skills, and they frequently are developmentally behind their nonchemically dependent sisters. Often they have experienced years of lost learning, as though, like Rip Van Winkle, they awaken in recovery to a world that has gone on without them. They cannot get those years back, and they must struggle to catch up. They are faced with the conflict between "making up for lost time" and recognizing where they are in their lives and going on from there. To do this, they must grieve their losses, accept the limitations in their lives, and discover the paths they need to follow on their physical, emotional, and spiritual quest for meaning and fulfillment.

REFERENCES

Bean, M. H. (1981). Denial and the psychological complications of alcoholism. In M. H. Bean, E. J. Khantzian, J. E. Mack, G. E. Vaillant, & N. E. Zinberg (Eds.), *Dynamic approaches to the understanding and treatment of alcoholism* (pp. 128-162). New York: Free Press.

Bennett, R. (1997, Spring). Some issues on transitions in midlife and older women: Stress, coping, and social supports. *The Renfrew Perspective, 3*(1), 15-17.

Finnegan, D. G., & McNally, E. B. (1996). Chemically dependent lesbians and bisexual women: Recovery from many traumas. *Journal of Chemical Dependency Treatment, 6*(1/2), 87-107.

Grice, D. E. (1994). *PTSD, victimization and substance abuse.* Manuscript submitted for publication.

Herman, J. L. (1992). *Trauma and recovery: The aftermath of violence–from domestic abuse to political terror.* New York: Basic Books.

Hull, J. G. (1987). Self-awareness model. In H. T. Blane & K. E. Leonard (Eds.), *Psychological theories of drinking and alcoholism* (pp. 272-304). New York: Guilford Press.

Kasl, C. D. (1993). *Many roads, one journey: Moving beyond the 12 steps.* New York: HarperCollins.

Khantzian, E. J. (1981). Some treatment implications of the ego and self disturbances in alcoholism. In M. H. Bean, E. J. Khantzian, J. E. Mack, G. E. Vaillant, & N. E. Zinberg (Eds.), *Dynamic approaches to the understanding and treatment of alcoholism* (pp. 128-162). New York: Free Press.

Krystal, H. (1988). *Integration & self-healing: Affect, trauma, alexithymia.* Hillsdale, NJ: Analytic Press.

Kus, R. J. (1988). Alcoholism and non-acceptance of gay self: The critical link. *Journal of Homosexuality, 15*(1/2), 25-41.

Lavender, J. (1997, Spring). "How could this have happened to me?": The phenomenology of the relational void. *The Renfrew Perspective, 3*(1), 12-15.

Mack, J. (1981). Alcoholism, AA, and the governance of the self. In M. H. Bean, E. J. Khantzian, J. E. Mack, G. E. Vaillant, & N. E. Zinberg (Eds.), *Dynamic approaches to the understanding and treatment of alcoholism* (pp. 128-162). New York: Free Press.

McNally, E. B. (1989). *Lesbian recovering alcoholics in Alcoholics Anonymous: A qualitative study of identity transformation.* Unpublished doctoral dissertation, New York University, New York.

Niemela, P., & Lento, R. (1993). The significance of the 50th birthday for women's individuation. In N. D. Davis, E. Cole, & E. D. Rothblum (Eds.), *Faces of women and aging* (pp. 117-127). Binghamton, NY: The Haworth Press, Inc.

Pandina, R. J. (1982). Effects of alcohol on psychological processes. In E. L. Gomberg, H. R. White, & J. A. Carpenter (Eds.), *Alcohol, science, and society revisited* (pp. 38-62). Ann Arbor: University of Michigan Press.

Pearlman, S. F. (1993). Late midlife astonishment: Disruptions to identity and self-esteem. In N. D. Davis, E. Cole, & E. D. Rothblum (Eds.), *Faces of women and aging* (pp. 1-12). Binghamton, NY: The Haworth Press, Inc.

Stein, M. (1983). *In midlife: A Jungian perspective.* Dallas: Spring Publications.

Weber, E. (1977). Incest begins at home. *MS* 5 (2 bound)(10 unbound), 64-67, 105.

Midlife Lesbian Parenting

Christa Donaldson

SUMMARY. This study explores the experience of nine midlife lesbian mothers parenting young children. The participants live in the greater Bay Area of San Francisco.

The participants reported positive feelings about their parenting experience. They felt confident and secure in midlife, and this enhanced their parenting. Their own maturation issues, whether they were coming out or other developmental concerns, seem successfully traversed, leaving them more inner resources for mothering.

Participants experienced acceptance from the larger culture, as well as discrimination and ignorance. Participants experienced little conflict regarding nurturing with their partner and little conflict with respect to their identities as mothers. *[Article copies available for a fee from The Haworth Document Delivery Service: 1-800-342-9678. E-mail address: <getinfo@haworthpressinc. com> Website: <http://www.haworthpressinc.com>]*

KEYWORDS. Lesbian, parenting, midlife, alternative parenting, female development, middle-aged parents, lesbian mothers

INTRODUCTION

Increasing numbers of lesbians are choosing to have children in the context of a preexisting lesbian identity (Patterson, 1994; Slater,

Christa Donaldson, PhD, is a clinical psychologist in private practice in Berkeley and San Francisco. Dr. Donaldson is the former director of the Feminist Therapy Graduate Program at Antioch University, San Francisco, California.

Christa Donaldson can be reached at 211 Vine Street, Berkeley, CA 94709.

[Haworth co-indexing entry note]: "Midlife Lesbian Parenting." Donaldson, Christa. Co-published simultaneously in *Journal of Gay & Lesbian Social Services* (Harrington Park Press, an imprint of The Haworth Press, Inc.) Vol. 11, No. 2/3, 2000, pp. 119-138; and: *Midlife Lesbian Relationships: Friends, Lovers, Children, and Parents* (ed: Marcy R. Adelman) Harrington Park Press, an imprint of The Haworth Press, Inc., 2000, pp. 119-138. Single or multiple copies of this article are available for a fee from The Haworth Document Delivery Service [1-800-342-9678, 9:00 a.m. - 5:00 p.m. (EST). E-mail address: getinfo@haworthpressinc.com].

1995). Within this diverse group, a small but significant number are midlife lesbians choosing to mother young children. This phenomenon is possible because of positive cultural changes in how lesbian mothers are viewed; the "lesbian baby boom," which provides peer support for lesbian mothers through increased visibility to one another; and increased life expectancy for this generation.

The midlife lesbian mother is also part of a larger trend of American women choosing to postpone child rearing. The lesbian mother uniquely has the opportunity to become the mother of a young child well past her actual childbearing years; an older lesbian coupled with a younger woman is not bound to motherhood by biology or the age limits placed on women through adoption policies.

While the children of lesbians often have been studied, little is known about lesbian mothers in general, or about midlife lesbian mothers in particular. This study explores the experience of nine midlife lesbian mothers parenting young children and how these mothers feel parenting, midlife issues, and sexual orientation interact to affect their lives.

HISTORICAL FACTORS

The phenomenon of midlife lesbians choosing to have children can be attributed to several converging political and socioeconomic factors. American women, in general, are choosing to have children later in life due both to the influence of the women's movement and an expanded sense of choice for middle-class women and the need for two wage earners to sustain a family. Many women are investing in their education and careers, establishing themselves in the work force before they have children.

The women's self-help health movement, as an outgrowth of the women's movement, demystified conception and fertility and provided women with information about donor insemination. As heterosexual women and lesbians became more informed, they began to exercise more control over procreation.

Additionally, the lesbian and gay rights movement has increased the number of options available to lesbians. Lesbians and gay men have challenged the limitations placed on their lives by insisting on being visible to the mainstream culture, and their increased visibility has eroded many homophobic stereotypes. There are more realistic images of lesbian and gay parents in the media; this provides gays and lesbians, themselves, with the notion that their sexual orientation and their desire to have children need not necessarily be at odds. With this shift in cultural attitudes toward lesbian parents, adoption, too, has become a viable option. International adoptions are increasingly popular in this country. This change has aided many lesbians in their bids to adopt.

All these trends have challenged the cultural imperatives of "compulsory" mothering for heterosexual women and "compulsory" childlessness for lesbians (Crawford, 1987). The generation of lesbians now in midlife is the first to benefit from these vast cultural shifts; many are choosing parenting either by adoption, birthing, or co-parenting as "out" lesbians.

Previous research in several areas bears on this study: midlife issues for women, the dynamics between lesbian couples, research on lesbian mothers, and the role community plays in the lives of lesbians. The most relevant research on these topics is summarized as an introduction to this study.

MIDLIFE

Midlife is seen increasingly as a time of great potential for women. Midlife women express more independence and know better who they are and what they want (Niemela & Lent, 1993). Today's life expectancy for women is approximately 80 years old. Midlife, therefore, is a viable component of a woman's total life span. The meaning in women's lives during midlife is constructed from primarily two sources: their relationships, especially those with other women (which increase in significance as women age), and attention to their own psychological and spiritual growth (Harrison, 1994).

Historically, where the heterosexual woman was discouraged from serious career aspirations, the lesbian assumed sole responsibility for her own economic survival. Some midlife lesbians emphasize fun in their lives after being primarily achievement oriented; some may have "midlife crises" in which external forces reshape their lives, and some make a conscious decision to do something different with their lives (Posen, 1991).

Lesbians already are stigmatized by the culture; they have little status to lose by aging. Furthermore, they very likely may have already developed a "crisis competence"; that is, coping strategies to deal with discrimination and prejudice (Kimmel, 1978). Often, in coming out, a lesbian faced disapproval and disdain from family, friends, and coworkers. In this painful process, she may gain fortitude and courage regarding her own choices; she might learn to value herself apart from the mandates of the culture. Perhaps this explains, in part, Bell's findings (1971) that lesbians find aging less traumatic than their heterosexual peers. One study found that lesbians, unlike heterosexual women, feel just as attractive, if not more attractive, in midlife than in their younger years (Almvig, 1982). The age of lesbians' partners is also not as important as in heterosexual relationships (Laner, 1979).

COMMUNITY

Within our culture, the meaning and structure of family varies among different subcultures. Research on lesbian lifestyle also indicates that lesbians tend to form extended networks of support that function like a large family (Lewin, 1981; Weston, 1991). These "family networks," formed with ex-lovers and other friends, often involve sharing "familial obligations" such as living together or sharing vehicles or child care/elder care (Weston, 1991). This "family" structure is similar to those kinship networks found in many indigent African-American families; kin are recognized as those who share socioeconomic obligations regardless of a lack of blood relationship (Stack, 1974; Weston, 1991).

LESBIAN RELATIONSHIPS

Salient issues for lesbians in relationships are power, dependency, nurturance, and "merging" (Burch, 1982, 1986). Although not unique to lesbian relationships, these dynamics tend to be intensified by the lack of prescribed social roles, the shared gender socialization, and the potentially equal status between women in relationship to one another.

Lesbian couples tend to strive for a balance of power within their relationships, emphasizing "fairness" and a sense of egalitarianism; thus, lesbian relationships tend to be more egalitarian than heterosexual relationships (Schneider, 1986; Taylor, 1980). Without the social roles prescribed to men and women, lesbian couples negotiate issues such as money, time, vacations, living arrangements, and division of labor regarding shared tasks within a context of mutuality (Caldwell & Peplau, 1984; Lynch & Reilly, 1986). The fact that women are socialized to be "nurturers" in intimate relationships creates an expectation of being nurtured in lesbian relationships. If the partners fail to meet each other's needs, conflict often arises (Burch, 1997).

Much has been written about merger in lesbian relationships (Burch, 1982; Burch, 1986). Lesbians' tendencies to blur distinctions between themselves and their partners is a product of women's facility with intimacy and fluid boundaries and their difficulty maintaining a sense of separate self in the face of another's needs (Burch, 1982; Burch, 1997). This dynamic may serve to enhance a relationship, or it may contribute to a loss of sense of self.

LESBIAN MOTHERS

Over the last 15 years, lesbian couples establishing families have provided researchers the opportunity to study the effects of lesbian parents on their children's development (Patterson, 1992, 1995). The resultant studies have found no differences in gender socialization of the children of lesbians and heterosexuals and no differences in the adjustment and psychological well-being of the mothers (Falk, 1989; Kleber, Howell, & Tibbits-Klebber, 1986; Martin, 1993; Paul, 1986; Slater, 1995).

The effect of having children upon lesbian couples has been the focus of several other studies (Donaldson, 1987; McCandish, 1987; Patterson, 1995; Stiglitz, 1990). Donaldson (1987) studied the experience of 12 lesbian couples who had chosen to parent a child together. Her findings seem to indicate that having children affects lesbian couples in several paradoxical ways. Sharing the "role" of mother (the tasks and responsibilities) seemed desirable, yet sharing the "identity" of mother (the affection, social role, and sense of primacy) was not desirable. A majority of the subjects described feeling competitive with their partners regarding their primacy with their children (Donaldson, 1987).

For lesbian mothers to share the identity of mother, each woman must make a deep psychological shift from an expectation of exclusive primacy to an experience of shared primacy. This shift is often a difficult achievement for these mothers, both because there is a dearth of models for two fully involved parents and because lesbians have been acculturated to believe that being a lesbian runs counter to being feminine, nurturing, or–in a word–a mother (Burch, 1997; Donaldson, 1987).

Burch (1997) offers a theoretical analysis of the lesbian family structure and parental dynamics in *Other Women, Lesbian/Bisexual Experience and Psychoanalytic Views of Women.* Her synthesis of research and theory captures the challenges a lesbian couple may encounter in forming a two-mother family not mirrored by main-stream culture nor supported by Western developmental psychological theory. She concludes that women are particularly well suited to managing the family triangle because so much of their early development is organized around maintaining relationships rather than around competition and conquest.

McCandish (1987) found that the lesbian mothers she studied experienced an increase in hostility in their relationship after the birth of a child, particularly around the issue of nurturance. Biological mothers often envied the freedom of their co-parent, while the co-parent felt envious of the close bond between mother and child. These women described a greater need for support and nurturance from their partners after the birth of their child and felt they were getting less of it than they had experienced before the birth.

Patterson's (1995) extensive research indicates differences in the roles assumed by the biological and the nonbiological lesbian mothers. The couples in her study reported sharing household responsibilities, including decision-making, equally, yet the biological mothers reported doing more child care and the nonbiological mothers reported spending longer hours at work. Patterson found that when lesbian couples shared child care more evenly, however, the mothers were more satisfied and the children were better adjusted.

Research on heterosexual families shows women do the majority of household maintenance and care of children (Cowan & Cowan, 1992; Kurdek, 1993). This finding persists even when the women also are employed outside the home; sociologist Hochschild (1989) labeled this the "second shift" for women.

As one might expect on the basis of the egalitarian ethic reflected in Patterson's lesbian couples' descriptions of ideal divisions of child care responsibilities, biological mothers were more satisfied when they did less, and nonbiological mothers were more satisfied when they did more than the average amount of child care. "Thus, even under pressure of child-rearing responsibilities, lesbian couples seem to maintain relatively egalitarian division of household responsibilities in a number of areas" (Patterson, 1995, p. 120).

PURPOSE

The purpose of the present study is to describe the experience of midlife lesbian mothers with young children. Do midlife lesbian mothers experience difficulties navigating issues of shared primacy with their partners? Are they able to adhere to egalitarian division of labor within their families? What are the salient issues for them as midlife parents? How do they feel their midlife issues affect their parenting of young children?

STUDY

Participants were all at least 45 years old, lesbian, the parent of a child eight years or younger, and in a relationship of at least three years' duration. The women who participated in this study all are currently living in the San Francisco Bay Area and San Jose. They were solicited through word of mouth. Each woman participated in an interview lasting between one and two hours.

METHOD

Is it reasonable or possible to speak in quantitative terms of the struggle for the formation of a socially and psychologically valued identity? Is the method and language of quantification best suited to research that seeks to understand a people's hopes, fears, values conflicts, struggles and above all their complex and often contradictory sense of themselves?

(Rubin, 1979, p. 225)

This phenomenological study was structured in such a way as to allow the maximum amount of flexibility in answering. Each participant was asked the same questions and given maximum flexibility in answering. The interviewer pursued each participant's responses to facilitate the emergence of unexpected issues.

Each interview was taped and the tapes were reviewed for themes and commonalties among the participants' experiences. An issue or experience was considered a common theme if four or more women discussed it.

SUBJECTS

A total of nine women participated in this study. The mean age of participants is 50.7 years, with a range from 45 to 62 years. Six women are Caucasian, two are African-American, and one is Hispanic. The class standing of the women is predominantly professional, middle class, and six of the women identify as having a professional career. Two women identify as working class; both of those women work in the trades. One woman who worked part-time also identified herself as blue-collar.

Each participant in the study has been in the same relationship with her partner for at least 5 years. The mean length of relationship is 11 years. The length of relationships ranged from 5 years to 16 years' duration. The age difference between participants and their partners ranged from 1 year to 19 years. The partners of the participants were not interviewed.

Of the nine study participants, eight are nonbiological mothers, six participants' partners carried their child, and two participants adopted children. One participant gave birth when she was 43 years old. Three of the participants in this study had had children previously: one as a single woman, one as a married woman, and one in a committed lesbian relationship. One participant had a son in his 20s, another had five grown children, and one had a teenage daughter still living at home.

The age range of the participants' 12 children is six weeks to eight years old; their mean age is 36.5 months. All the children's development, as of the time of the study, has been normal; none have presented any unusual challenges to normal parent-child bonding.

	Age	Race	Work Status	Length of Relationship	Relationship to Child
Participant #1	53	African-American	full-time	7 years	nonbiological
Participant #2	49	African-American	full-time	5 years	biological
Participant #3	45	Caucasian	full-time	12 years	adoptive
Participant #4	62	Hispanic	full-time	14 years	nonbiological
Participant #5	46	Caucasian	full-time	12 years	adoptive
Participant #6	49	Caucasian	full-time	13 years	nonbiological
Participant #7	52	Caucasian	half-time	16 years	nonbiological
Participant #8	53	Caucasian	full-time	10 years	nonbiological
Participant #9	45	Caucasian	full-time	12.5 years	nonbiological

The table above summarizes the demographic information regarding age, race, work status, length of relationship to co-parent, and relationship to the child.

RESULTS

All the participants reported positive feelings about their parenting experience. In general, they felt confident and secure in midlife, and this enhanced their parenting. "I might have had more energy when I was younger, but I didn't really know myself–my capabilities and my weaknesses. I also feel like I have a much better handle on things now, so I see my age as a benefit and not a limit to my parenting," one participant reflected. The three participants who previously had children felt that the older they became, the more they were able to parent effectively.

All participants describe feeling competent as mothers and bonded with their children. Six of them felt their age allowed them to be "more mellow," six felt they were more resourceful, and seven felt they were more patient with their children than they imagined they would have been had they become mothers at a younger age. "Less of my own wildness gets in the mix when I'm dealing with my kid's acting out," says a 48-year-old mother with a 6-year-old child. "My coming out and my kid's freaking out definitely would have conflicted for center stage if I had kids earlier," another participant commented.

Five participants discussed feeling "challenged" by sharing with their co-parent a sense of primacy with their child. "I find myself simultaneously appreciating and resenting my girlfriend's relationship to our daughter," said a participant. Another expressed concern: "Will the baby be able to handle all this love? After all, if I focus on him all morning, then my partner comes home and she dotes all afternoon while I'm at work, isn't he going to get sick of one of us?" "I want him all to myself sometimes. Even though I have actual time alone with him, I worry that my partner is more important to him because she's the biological mom," stated another participant.

Seven participants report being as involved in the mothering experience as their co-parents. In particular, the five participants whose partners initially nursed their babies felt this determined the roles each parent played more than age did. These participants did not feel that they had any less energy than their partners, although several couples had age differences of 10 years or more. The nonbiological mothers reported having a great deal of energy and enthusiasm for the non-nursing child care tasks and activities. Once past the nursing stage, as for the two adoptive parents, seven participants described "divvying up tasks and responsibilities based on preference, time considerations, family expediency, and economic realities." Six participants felt that they do the same amount of child care and household tasks as their partners.

Of the two who described an unequal investment of time and energy, one of the participants who said that equal parenting had been her original intention described herself as being more in a "father's role." She felt that she had not anticipated just how much "creative energy parenting would take" from her, and she felt too depleted by parenting to successfully complete her own creative work. Her partner, she felt, understood her dilemma and felt "no resentment." The other participant who felt she did slightly less parenting than her partner negotiated this arrangement with her partner before the birth of their daughter. She felt that "at my age, if I am to pull this off, I'm going to need several long vacations a year, time to myself, and the permission to beg off on middle-of-the-night feedings now and then."

All the participants reported a lessening of romantic and sexual intimacy between themselves and their partners and a realignment of interests in family activities following the birth or adoption of a child. This emphasis on children and family tended to have shifted back to increased intimacy for the couples whose children had entered school and with each passing year.

The intimacy experienced with the child became desired and sought after, often even when the partner/co-parent might have been available for intimate contact. "I guess if I had to choose, I'd spend time with my son at this point, and I think my girlfriend would do the same," answered one participant when asked about intimacy needs. Five other women voiced similar feelings.

Participants spoke about the lack of "grown-up intimate time," as one woman labeled her adult intimate sexual relationship. Although there was quite a bit of joking about the dearth of intimate time together, most of these participants did not express serious unhappiness about the state of their romantic relationships with their partners. One participant described that, while watching her partner with their baby, she felt "held and loved by proxy." Another reported that "watching just how loving my girlfriend is with the kids draws me in; I feel enveloped."

Seven of the participants raised issues of greater contact with the mainstream community since having children; five of these participants felt that they were more comfortable straddling the fence between the lesbian community and the dominant mainstream culture than they would have been when younger.

Six women reported feeling more confident dealing with prejudice from community institutions (such as schools, doctors, or hospitals) than they had been when they were younger. Five of the participants recounted negative experiences in the larger community. One described "a nosy neighbor asking my son about his father or where he came from." Another talked about being told "There can't be two mothers. Which is the 'real' mother?" These five women feared the effects of such experiences on their children.

Yet many of these same participants and several more reported "being pleasantly surprised at the amount of acceptance" they had found in the larger community. They described needing to "educate the various child care facilities we've used" regarding lesbian lifestyle or "Who calls whom what?"as one participant characterized the confusion often encountered regarding parental terminology. Two participants recounted recent incidents of discrimination toward them as lesbian mothers, yet they chose to minimize these incidents in the face of "so much acceptance and curiosity, at worst." This curiosity affected several other participants differently. "I know that I've faced far worse in my lifetime, but I don't want my kids to suffer any of it," one participant said.

Six of the nine participants described being very involved in all aspects of their children's contact with the larger community as a way to either "help educate other parents to who we actually are as lesbian moms" or to "watch out for my kids. If anyone has any weird questions about how they came to be, I can answer them, and my kids won't have to."

It is interesting to note that five of the women interviewed initially felt, upon coming out, that their lesbianism conflicted with their desire to have children. "I always wanted kids, but I thought that was not possible once I came out. I didn't really think it through; I just couldn't put it together with being gay. It's funny, because now it seems like the best of both worlds; but at 24, I didn't have any role models."

When asked to describe other concerns regarding being older lesbian mothers, six participants described being afraid that their children's peers would mistake them for grandmothers, rather than mothers. (This had not happened.) Five participants said they had feared not "having the energy" for young children. This fear had not been borne out. When asked to describe the positive aspects of parenting as a midlife lesbian, seven participants described the closeness that developed or deepened with their co-parent and partner. One participant's articulation captures the spirit of what these women were describing. She stated, "I felt a deepening of appreciation, love, and respect for my partner that evolved, I think, from that close and constant team-work that having a baby has required of us."

Seven of the participants also described the overwhelming support they have received from their extended "family of friends" and from their biological families. "It takes more than a village," as one woman said, "to deal with balancing sick kids, work and shopping, dinner—those sort of things. I could never do it alone and I wouldn't want to, because part of my social contact comes from my friends' involvement in our family." She, and other participants, describes friends and family providing emotional support as well as helping pick children up at school, feeding children dinner, etc. Several women said that their ex-lovers were a central support in their present family endeavor.

Most couples had made mutual decisions regarding how to balance childcare needs and economic realities. The decision for one partner to work part-time and therefore be more available for their child's needs came easily to several couples; two others finally agreed to this arrangement, but only after significant conflict about it. Two high-wage earning participants reluctantly accepted advancement in their work after the birth/adoption of their child, yet they felt ambivalent about the increased demands of their jobs. They described their decisions to accept advancement as being based solely on the family's economic needs and not as an investment in their careers.

Three subjects reported that they and their partners worked part-time since the birth or adoption of their children. This was experienced both as an accommodation to the children's needs and as satisfying the need to spend more time with their children.

Fears about economic security and their children's growing economic needs weighed heavily on all the women. "Retirement and college costs are going to collide for me, and I worry about it all the time," said one 48-year-old mother of a very young child. Although there are large economic differences between the couples, in terms of class background, class standing, and what several women stood to inherit, the fears about being able to adequately provide for their children existed regardless of financial circumstances.

Five women raised concerns about their elderly parents. Each felt a dual responsibility to care both for their child or children and their parents. One woman received an emergency call regarding her mother's failing health during the interview and was in the process of making arrangements for her mother's care at the same time she was home with two young children. Another woman in the study recently asked her aging mother to live with her, her children, and her partner.

Five women voiced the fear of being unable to be a full participant in their children's continuing development. They were concerned that they, unlike their own parents, would not be in good health when it came time for their children to graduate, marry, or have children of their own.

DISCUSSION

The participants' descriptions of mothering in midlife were overwhelmingly positive. Most participants felt that they have reached a new level of patience and confidence in midlife, which has enhanced their parenting. Participants' maturation issues, whether these be "coming out" or other concerns, seem successfully traversed, leaving them with more inner resources for the task of mothering.

These participants have chosen to have children at a time when many midlife women are facing the "empty nest." Women who followed the traditional life trajectory had children at an age that leaves them in middle age with the time to discover parts of their identities that had been put on hold. A case might be made that that is precisely what the midlife lesbian mother is doing. Social and psychological restrictions did not allow many of these women to entertain the idea of motherhood until midlife. The participants have chosen a unique and satisfying midlife expression of their hard-won freedom to choose, certainly made possible by the increased acceptance of lesbians and gay men in the culture and the increase in life expectancy for their generation.

Furthermore, young women coming of age in the late 1940s and 1950s would have images perpetuated by the culture of gay men and lesbians living lonely destitute lives, devoid of family and supportive social contacts. Perhaps this "shadow" still plays a part in terms of the anxiety and preoccupation these women exhibit regarding issues of financial insecurities, anticipated loss of parents, and inability to imagine retirement.

The formative years of the majority of these women were such that the cultural images of lesbians they encountered were pejorative. That most women did not have the psychological wherewithal to undertake the venture of children without men speaks to the psychological parameters that a culture places on one's ability to envision freedom from those cultural strictures.

These midlife lesbians felt "thrown into the mainstream," as one participant put it, by having a child; they felt both more visible to the mainstream culture and more invisible in many ways. The participants described being asked insensitive or ignorant questions regarding their family that served to make them feel concerned for their children.

Compared to younger lesbian mothers (mean age 36 years old) studied earlier (Donaldson, 1987), the midlife lesbian mothers (mean age 50.7 years old) in this study experienced less conflict within themselves and with their partners with respect to their identities as mother. It was a significant part of the younger lesbians' experiences as new mothers, both nonbiological and biological, to feel threatened by the primacy of their co-parents. By contrast, there seemed to be less "felt" imbalance of power vis-à-vis the baby for the midlife lesbian mother than that experienced by the younger lesbian mother. It should be noted that the midlife mothers in the present study are primarily nonbiological mothers.

The participants in this study describe the experience of the child demonstrating a preference for one or the other mother at times, but it did not have the valence for these midlife mothers that it had for the younger lesbian mothers (Donaldson, 1987). The older lesbian mothers also reported much less competitive "tug of war" with their co-parent for the affection of the child than the younger lesbians (mean age 36 years old) had. Perhaps these older women, although aware of the challenge of sharing primacy with their co-parent, do not have the same driving need for validation from their child that the younger lesbians expressed. Previous research on younger lesbian mothers does indicate a vying for the primary identity of mother, which could lead one to believe that the lack of competition in the older lesbian mother is, in fact, a function of age. It seems the lack of competition experienced by these women compared to their younger counterparts (Donaldson, 1987) can be attributed to the fact that the older parent is no longer striving to "prove herself." This finding would be consistent with what we know about women at midlife in general. This may be a function of having fewer questions about one's identity in midlife (Niemela & Lent, 1993).

Having a child both exacerbated and alleviated the issue of merger between study participants and their partners. A majority of the women described being far more aware of every aspect of their partner's life since sharing the responsibility of a child. At the same time, these women report feeling much more merged with their children than with their partners. It would seem, as with the younger lesbian mothers (Donaldson, 1987), that the family triad in a lesbian household has both parents riveted on the child. The competition, when it exists, is for the child's affection or for a sense of primacy with the child, not necessarily intimacy with the other parent. This is in contrast to heterosexual households, where the father often remains more bonded to his partner and the mother feels primarily merged or attached to the child. Either dynamic can become problematic if intensified by other issues, such as a lack of bond with the child for either parent or the lack of any adult intimate relationship. There are potential pitfalls in either constellation; for the lesbian couple, it may also create "a sense that there's not enough baby to go around, or there's too much baby and not enough attention to the adult relationship" (Donaldson, 1987).

None of the participants expressed serious concerns for the state of the intimate, sexual relationship with her partner. This could be interpreted as a mature, confident position where the women realize that the needs of the children will dominate the family initially; however, several studies have indicated that lesbian mothers sometimes subsume their own adult intimacy needs to such an extent that they are difficult to resuscitate (Donaldson, 1987; Stiglitz, 1990).

The division of labor within a lesbian household with children is a source of "endless discussion" as one participant put it. The midlife lesbian mothers in this study described negotiating agreements with partners about household chores before they had children; yet they acknowledged that once they actually had children, these finely honed distinctions and roles evaporated.

This finding is consistent with Patterson's (1995) finding that in lesbian families, after the birth of a child, the parents' roles became somewhat specialized, despite their original intentions to share child care tasks equally. The less the disparity between the couple regarding child care, however, the greater satisfaction the partners experience in a lesbian relationship (Patterson, 1995), which is consistent with the egalitarian values espoused by lesbian couples in general. Nursing, initially, dictated roles of the mothers, yet once the biological mother stopped nursing, these midlife mothers reported an "equalizing effect," as one participant called it. They described divvying up tasks according to expedience. The lack of socially prescribed roles according to gender and the shared gender socialization for these lesbian mothers seem to ameliorate the possibility of a "second shift" phenomenon that many heterosexual working mothers experience.

The high degree of mutuality and willingness to process in lesbian couples seems to be in evidence with these participants. They, for the most part, successfully (defined by their own satisfaction) negotiated financial arrangements, child care schedules, and division of labor. It must be taken into account that the purpose and scope of this research did not include an interview with each participant's partner. Since the partners were overwhelmingly the biological mothers, it is possible that their experiences would be quite different than the participants'.

Most of the subjects in this study are of a generation that has aging or elderly parents still living. These women, for the most part, are part of the postwar baby boom, and their own parents were quite young when they had children. They now face a decidedly different experience with their own children. Even though life expectancy is longer than any other time in history, these women have had their children at an age that determines that they will no longer be living when their children are the age they are now. Many expressed deep grief at the loss for both themselves and their children that they could not safely assume they would be alive to see their children through the many "rites of passage" of adulthood. These fears reflect, in part, the important role their parents played at milestone events in their own lives. Many of the same women who voiced this concern spoke often of memories of their own parents' involvement in so much of their lives.

There is a great deal of economic uncertainty in the baby boomer generation, and certainly for the one participant who lived through the Depression years in this country. This tendency to worry about the future and Social Security benefits, retirement, and college costs seems exacerbated by these all happening simultaneously. Furthermore, women-headed households generally have much greater economic limitations.

Lesbians always have faced the prospect of supporting themselves economically. As noted earlier, lesbians traditionally faced the culture mandate of childlessness, yet were "permitted" careers. Many of these women have had no other financial support throughout the years; this economic independence is not a new responsibility, yet cultural images of destitute lesbians and gay men aging alone may persist to fuel much of the anxiety expressed by these women.

"Crisis competence," gender role flexibility, and a broad definition of family seemed to contribute to the positive experience these women had as middle-aged lesbian mothers with young children. They felt that they dealt effectively and directly with discrimination, yet minimized it in the face of all the "acceptances" they experienced. This may speak, again, to the "shadow"; that is, their expectations based on their formative experiences may be low in terms of social acceptance and equitable treatment from cultural institutions. An enormous cultural shift has taken place in their lifetime. These women may experience both the benefits of that shift and still carry the psychological underpinnings of some more repressive cultural milieu.

This study is based on a small, geographically clustered group of midlife lesbian mothers. All of the participants live in the San Francisco Bay Area and San Jose, two areas of the country whose residents pride themselves on acceptance and services for lesbians and gay men. Both this and the size of the study must be kept in mind when extrapolating from the results.

IMPLICATIONS FOR TREATMENT

It may be tempting for the clinician who treats midlife lesbian mothers and/or their families to focus on the relative ease with which these women chose to have families or the "acceptance" these women report; yet it is crucial to listen closely to what else these women experience. The added burden of discrimination or having their families treated as a novelty adds stress to the already stressful situation of parenting. Furthermore, the midlife lesbian mother may find herself falling between the parenting community and the lesbian community. By dint of their age, these midlife lesbian mothers may have little in common with other new parents, independent of sexual orientation.

These women bring a great deal of competence and confidence to their new endeavor of raising a child, yet they might tend to minimize the burdens of parenthood. There seems to be little room for "marginalized" parents to share the feelings of being overwhelmed or stressed by their choice to have children. Although this might be true for all lesbian and gay parents, it might have particular relevance for the midlife lesbian mother in that she is expected to "know her own mind and to make good choices," as one participant said.

Finally, as with lesbian parents in general, the issue of "too much focus on the baby, not enough on the couple" is a common problem. Again, this is a natural and well-documented tendency with new parents. With lesbian parents, the couple might need help redirecting energy and vitality into the adult relationship after the newness of becoming parents wears off. A balance is difficult to achieve, especially if the parents feel that they are exercising a privilege they never thought they would have, as is true for many midlife lesbian mothers.

REFERENCES

Almvig, C. (1982). *The invisible minority: Aging and lesbianism.* New York.. Utica College of Syracuse University Press.

Bell, R. (1971). *Social deviance.* Homewood, IL: Dorsey Press.

Burch, B. (1982). Psychological merger in lesbian couples: A joint ego psychological and systems approach. *Family Therapy,* 201.

Burch, B. (1986). Psychotherapy and the dynamics of merger in lesbian couples. In C. Cohen and T. Stein (Eds.), *Psychotherapy with gay men and lesbians.* New York: Plenum.

Burch, B. (1997). *Other women: Lesbian/bisexual experience and psychoanalytic views of women.* New York: Columbia University Press.

Caldwell, M., & Peplau, L. (1984). The balance of power in lesbian relationships. *Sex Roles, 10,* 587-599.

Cowan, C., & Cowan, P. (1992). *When partners become parents: The big life change for couples.* New York: Basic Books.

Crawford, S. (1987). Lesbian families: Psychosocial stress and the family building process. In Boston Lesbian Psychologies Collective (Eds.), *Lesbian psychologies, exploration and challenges.* Urbana and Chicago: University of Illinois Press.

Donaldson, C. (1987). *The effects of sharing parenting on lesbian couples.* Paper presented at the Orthopsychiatry Conference, 1988, San Francisco; presented at American Psychiatric Association Conference, May 1990, New Orleans.

Falk, P. (1989). Lesbian mothers, psychosocial assumptions in family law. *American Psychologist, 44,* 941-947.

Harrison, C. (1994). *Aging and women's search for meaning after midlife.* Unpublished doctoral dissertation, Claremont Graduate School, CA, p. 234.

Hochschild, A. (1989). *The second shift: Working parents and the revolution at home.* New York: Viking Penguin.

Kimmel, D. (1978). Adult development and aging: A gay perspective. *Journal of Social Issues, 34,* 113-130.

Kleber, Howell, & Tibbits-Klebber (1986). The impact of parental homosexuality in child custody: A review of the literature. *Bulletin of American Academy of Psychiatry and Law, 14,* 81-87.

Kurdek, L. (1993). The allocation of household labor in homosexual and heterosexual cohabiting couples. *Journal of Social Issues, 49,* 127-139.

Laner, M. R. (1979). Growing older female: Heterosexual and homosexual. *Journal of Homosexuality, 4,* 267-273.

Lewin, E. (1981). Lesbianism and motherhood. *Human Organization, 40,* 6-14.

Lynch J., & Reilly, M. E. (1986). Role relationships: Lesbian perspectives. *Journal of Homosexuality, 12,* 53-69.

Martin, A. (1993). *The lesbian and gay parenting handbook.* New York: Harper.

McCandish, P. (1987). Against all odds: Lesbian mother family dynamics. In F. Bozett (Ed.). *Gay and lesbian parents* (pp. 23-38). New York: Praeger.

Niemela, P., & Lento, R. (1993). The significance of the 50th birthday for women's individuation. In N. Davis, E. Cole, & E. Rothblum (Eds.), *Faces of women and aging* (pp. 117-128). New York, London, and Norwood: The Haworth Press, Inc.

Patterson, C. (1992). Children of lesbian and gay parents. *Child Development, 63,* 1025-1042.

Patterson, C. (1994). Children and the lesbian baby boom: Behavioral adjustment, self-concepts, and sex role identity. In B. Greene & G. Herek (Eds.), *Contemporary perspectives on lesbian and gay psychology: Theory, research and application* (pp. 156-175). Beverly Hills, CA: Sage.

Patterson, C. (1995). Families of the lesbian baby boom: Parents' division of labor and children's adjustment. *Developmental Psychology, 31* (1), 115-123.

Paul, J. (1986). *Growing up with a gay, lesbian or bisexual parent: An exploratory study of experiences and perceptions.* Ann Arbor: UMI Dissertation Information Service.

Posen, P. (1991). Ripening. In B. Sang, J. Warshow, & A. Smith (Eds.), *Lesbians at midlife: The creative transition* (pp. 143-146). San Francisco: Spinsters Book Company.

Rubin, L. (1979). *Women of a certain age: The midlife search of self.* New York: Harper & Row.

Schneider, M. (1986). The relationship of cohabiting lesbian and heterosexual couples: A comparison. *Psychology of Women Quarterly, 10,* 234-239.

Slater, S. (1995). *The lesbian family life cycle.* New York: Free Press.

Stack, C. (1974). *All our kin: Strategies for survival in a black community.* New York: Harper Colophon.

Stiglitz, E. (1990). Caught between two worlds: The impact of a child on a lesbian couple's relationship. *Women & Therapy.* New York: The Haworth Press, Inc.

Taylor, V. (1980). Review essays of four books on lesbianism. *Journal of Marriage and the Family, 42,* 224-228.

Weston, K. (1991). *Families we choose.* New York: Columbia University Press.

Family Support Patterns
for Midlife Lesbians:
Recollections of a Lesbian Couple
1971-1997

Sharon M. Raphael
Mina K. Meyer

SUMMARY. The authors, an "out" lesbian couple, address the topic of support and nonsupport patterns as they apply to their own extended families over a 26-year period. As the family members age, interaction between the lesbian couple and the family appears to increase. An examination of the midlife lesbian's relationship with family of origin, particularly the mother-lesbian daughter bond, is discussed. Service providers are encouraged to pay special attention to the degree of acceptance and the quality of ties and interaction patterns that occur for later life mother-daughter relationships among "out" and "closeted" lesbians. *[Article copies available for a fee from The Haworth Document Delivery Service: 1-800-342-9678. E-mail address: <getinfo@haworthpressinc.com> Website: <http://www.haworthpressinc.com>]*

Sharon M. Raphael, PhD, is Professor of Sociology and Coordinator of the Graduate Behavioral Science Gerontology Option at California State University Dominguez Hills in Carson, California. Dr. Raphael is faculty advisor to both the Older Adult Center and the Gay, Lesbian, Bisexual Student Association. Mina K. Meyer, MA, is the Senior Human Relations Commissioner for the city of Long Beach, California.

Sharon M. Raphael, PhD, and Mina K. Meyer, MA, can be reached at 3735 Albury Avenue, Long Beach, CA 90808-2102.

[Haworth co-indexing entry note]: "Family Support Patterns for Midlife Lesbians: Recollections of a Lesbian Couple 1971-1997." Raphael, Sharon M., and Mina K. Meyer. Co-published simultaneously in *Journal of Gay & Lesbian Social Services* (Harrington Park Press, an imprint of The Haworth Press, Inc.) Vol. 11, No. 2/3, 2000, pp. 139-151; and: *Midlife Lesbian Relationships: Friends, Lovers, Children, and Parents* (ed: Marcy R. Adelman) Harrington Park Press, an imprint of The Haworth Press, Inc., 2000, pp. 139-151. Single or multiple copies of this article are available for a fee from The Haworth Document Delivery Service [1-800-342-9678, 9:00 a.m. - 5:00 p.m. (EST). E-mail address: getinfo@haworthpressinc.com].

139

KEYWORDS. Lesbian, family support, midlife, caretaking, lesbian daughter-mother relationship, life span development, lesbian family

This article reviews the personal history of a lesbian couple's relationship with their parents over the last three politically turbulent decades in an attempt to provide a clearer picture of family relationship and patterns of support for midlife lesbians. The question posed in the following personal and anecdotal recollection is where do "out" lesbians fit into the larger picture of family exchange and support across the life cycle, especially as it relates to caretaking of elderly parents? The following is not an answer, only a very preliminary attempt to raise the question about this under-researched topic.

This paper is conceptually based on the research of Ethel Shanas, Peter Townsend, and Jan Stehouwer, who conducted cross-cultural studies on relationships with extended families among old people in urban society and concluded that the family system was more intact and functional as people aged than previously assumed (Shanas, Townsend, & Stehouwer, 1968). Marvin Sussman's research on family systems and bureaucracy also contributed significantly to the premise that the extended family exchanged many goods and services across the generations in spite of the persistent stereotyped notion that the extended family is in a state of disintegration (Shanas & Sussman, 1977; Sussman & Steinmetz, 1987).

The literature on aging and family relationships posits a pattern of mothers turning to their daughters for emotional support (Abel, 1991) and of midlife daughters becoming caretakers (Norris, 1988; Somers & Shields, 1987). How lesbian relationships with their families of origin change over time and into midlife, and how being lesbian affects this pattern of mothers increasingly relying on their daughters and turning to their daughters for caretaking in later life, is an important area of study we hope to address.

The midlife lesbian's relationship with her family of origin is rarely described or studied. Warshow (1991), in her poignant description of her changed relationship with her dying mother after she came out to her, wrote, " . . . a lesbian having a parent accept her lifestyle and her partner makes a tremendous difference in whether the caregiving is obligatory or part of an ongoing positive relationship" (p. 72).

Meyer (1979), in a study of "closeted" middle-aged lesbians 10 years after Stonewall, reported that closeted daughters were typically perceived by their families as single women who were expected to care for their aging mothers. The closeted lesbians, in turn, willingly assumed the role of caretaker. Some women moved out of the home they shared with their lover and into the home of their mother. In more than a few instances, this meant a geographic move of some distance to another city or town. They would speak on the phone to their lover and visit when they could but felt their primary duty was to their mother. Other respondents moved the mother in with them and moved their lover either to another room or out of the house entirely until the mother died and the women could resume their lives as before.

Susan Johnson (1990), in a study on long-term lesbian couples, described wide variations in the kinds of relationships long-term couples had with their parents–from being open and supportive to being closed and closeted and offering little or no support. Yet she also reported a good number of lesbians who had taken on a caretaker role with their aging mother.

Midlife lesbians and their relationships with members of their families of origin are uniquely affected by the sociohistorical changes that they lived through that so radically altered society's perception and treatment of lesbians. For the gay/lesbian generations prior to Stonewall, disclosure to family, if attempted at all, was typically met with lifelong rejection (Adelman, 1991; Berger, 1982; Raphael & Robinson, 1984).

Today's midlife lesbians are the post-Stonewall generation who, more often than not, disclosed their lesbianism at the same time that traditional values and ideology regarding gay people were being challenged in the courts, in the media, and in the streets. According to Brown (1988) and Strommen (1989), there is no uniform response to the disclosure of a gay or lesbian family member. But the increasingly positive social acceptance of lesbianism assists the family, over time, to come to terms with their lesbian children.

Homophobia shapes both the process of the lesbian daughter's self-acceptance of her gay identity and the family's reaction to disclosure of her sexual orientation. Both daughter and family require time to adjust to a positive redefinition of the meanings and attitudes about lesbians (Cass, 1984; DeVine, 1984; Strommen, 1989).

In coming-out literature, there are various theories of sequential stages in gay/lesbian development (Cass, 1984; Plummer, 1975; Weinberg, 1983). Progress through stages can take several years or a lifetime to accomplish (Minnigerode & Adelman, 1978; Adelman, 1991). Delays in development can be understood as time to reassess negative attitudes about gay and lesbian people and homosexuality (DeMonteflores & Schultz, 1978), differences in idiosyncratic coping responses to external and internal homophobia (Adelman, 1991), and, or differences in class, race, and ethnicity (Greene, 1994).

DeVine (1984) described the process the family progresses through as a series of stages: (a) subliminal awareness, (b) impact, (c) adjustment, (d) resolution, and (e) integration. The family also needs time to mourn the loss of the old role the lesbian member played in the family and time to accept a new role for the lesbian member to take on after coming out (Strommen, 1990). Initial disclosure or discovery of sexual orientation brings on what Strommen (1990) labeled as the "revelation crisis," a short-lived period of intense internal and/or external conflict in the family. After this initial reaction to disclosure the family settles in to the often long progress through stages to integration. This process may take a lifetime to achieve, if achieved at all.

A poignant documentary movie (Hoffman, 1994) about a midlife lesbian daughter's relationship with her mother who has Alzheimer's disease reveals how the loss of memory allows a loving relationship to develop between a mother and a daughter and her life partner, based solely on her perception of how people relate to her and care for her rather than on the knowledge of who they are and how they are related. The loss of memory is bittersweet: it brings hardship and a constriction of life, but at the same time the loss of expectations and roles allows the emergence of a new constellation of nurturing relationships.

The authors, who are the subject of this study, "came out" in 1971 at the height of the gay/lesbian liberation movement and were highly involved in the gay liberation movement and feminist activities in the early 1970s. The authors describe their own situations as lesbians who are out to family and how they and their families of origin have related over the 26-year period described in this article.

For the purpose of clarifying to the reader who is who and which families are being described, the authors of this article will use their real first names to begin each account. Mina's family of origin in 1971 consisted of both parents and a brother who is 5 years younger. Sharon's family consisted of both parents and a brother who is 10 years older. In addition, Sharon has several aunts and uncles, first cousins, and a niece and nephew with whom she has contact. Mina has many aunts and many first cousins with whom she has regular interaction. At the present time, in 1997, both of Sharon's parents have died and Mina's father has died.

The following recollections were purposefully selected to show the relationship of emotional, social, and economic support or nonsupport between two generations of extended family members across a 26-year span of time. The authors write from the frame of reference of two "out" white lesbians who are in their 26-year relationship with each other.

CHRONOLOGY OF RECOLLECTIONS (1971-1997)

1971: Mina and Sharon meet by happenstance for the first time as adults in California and begin their relationship. Within a few days, Mina moves into Sharon's place. It should be noted that Mina and Sharon knew each other as children back in the 1940s but had not seen each other for 20 years at the time of this meeting. Sharon was 30 years of age and Mina was 31 years of age when they formed their adult relationship.

1971: Sharon had already "come out" with her mother. Her mother is clearly not happy about her daughter's lesbianism and does not tell her husband or other members of the family.

1972: Mina and Sharon "come out" to Mina's mother at a dinner. She cries and appears generally uncomfortable with the topic of lesbianism. When she gets home, she tells her husband. On the phone, she tells Mina that she does not want their relatives to know about her and Sharon.

1973: On a trip to visit Mina's parents, Mina and Sharon attend a holiday gathering at friends of Mina's parents. Mina's father introduces Mina and Sharon as "my daughter and my daughter-in-law." Mina and Sharon are shocked and delighted by this development.

1974: Mina and Sharon take a trip to see Sharon's family and to "come out" to Sharon's father. He is taken aback and confused. He inquires hostilely about what lesbians do in bed. Sharon's mother comes undone in an explosion of accusations and emotions. Voices are raised all around. The encounter ends when Mina and Sharon, angry and distraught, abruptly leave the house. The whole family gets caught up in the storm of feeling that will last more than two decades. When

Sharon's brother hears from their parents about her disclosure to them, he is angry and protective of the parents. In the midst of all this chaos, the issue of disinheritance is raised. Sharon tells her parents they can keep their money.

1975: Mina receives a note in the mail from her mother that a first cousin is teaching a course at a university on women and film. Mina, who has not seen this cousin since the cousin was seven years old, writes a "coming out" letter to her. The cousin responded with a "coming out" letter of her own. The cousin, who is planning to disclose to her own parents, asks if she would ask Mina's mother to contact her parents to give them support around this issue after she "comes out" to them. Mina's mother responds with an absolute "no." She tells Mina she had to deal with the issue by herself, and so her brother and her sister-in-law can do the same thing. Mina and Sharon continue to have a close and loving relationship with Mina's cousin, the cousin's life mate, and their adopted daughter.

1976: Mina's aunt on her father's side sends Sharon a birthday card that begins with the words "Dear Niece." She sends a card for Valentine's Day that begins with the words "Dear Nieces." She continues to send similar kinds of greetings to the present day.

1985: Mina's parents join a temple with a congregation consisting primarily of older adults. They become very active members. Mina and Sharon are very interested and curious about the temple but are not invited to attend or to go to any of the functions or socials that include temple members and their families and friends. Mina and Sharon assume this is because Mina's parents do not want the congregation to know the two are lesbians.

1987: The *Los Angeles Times* printed a Valentine's Day feature article titled, "Love Stories," which, for the first time, included a lesbian couple in addition to several heterosexual couples. Mina and Sharon are the lesbian couple in the article. About a month later, one of Mina's maternal aunts, who lives out of state, mentioned during a phone call that a California friend of hers sent her the article and that she thought "it was just lovely." (See article below.) Mina and Sharon were moved and delighted with her reaction. Today, in her mid-90s, this aunt never fails to ask about Sharon when Mina talks with her. Mina and Sharon visit her whenever possible.

Los Angeles Times, February 13, 1987

VIEW - TRENDS

LOVE STORIES

At Long Last Love

Relationships were uncomplicated for Mina Meyer back in _____. Her pals were the kids who lived on her block; children who hung out elsewhere were simply not in the running. So it was natural that Meyer, at age 7, became fast friends with Sharon Raphael, the 5-year-old across the street who was usually seen in Buster Brown loafers with white socks.

The girls road bicycles and played jacks, and together they faced up to the painful realization that their straight dark hair was just never going to be curly. Their relationship was smooth—until Mina moved away at age 12 and Sharon lost her older friend, her confidante.

Twenty years later, life was more complex. Mina had been through a marriage and a divorce and was dating a new man. She was breakfasting with her boyfriend one morning at a cafe in _____ where she was then living. An attractive, dark-haired woman approached her from across the diner and said, "Aren't you Mina Meyer from _____?"

Sure enough, it was Sharon-of-the-Buster-Browns. The two exchanged phone numbers and briefly caught up on school, career, and love histories. When Sharon said, "I'm not married and I'm never getting married," Mina had an idea what Sharon was talking about.

This Valentine's Day will be the 15th that Mina Meyer and Sharon Raphael have celebrated as a couple. Raphael, 45, is a professor of sociology at Cal State Dominguez Hills. Meyer, 47, teaches part time in the university's graduate gerontology program.

The two occasionally make trips back to _____ to visit family. And sometimes Sharon's mother still tells of the time the girl across the street moved, and how young Sharon stared out the window for a long time after her best friend drove away.

–Ann Japenga

1989: Mina is very upset because the temple had a celebration in honor of Mina's parents' 50th anniversary, and Mina and Sharon not only were not invited, but also were rebuffed by her parents when asked to be included. Mina and Sharon did celebrate the anniversary with them later along with Mina's brother and sister-in-law in Las Vegas.

1990: Sharon's parents come to Los Angeles for the first time to visit. Sharon and Mina show them around like tourists, and they have a good time. Sharon's father seems to enjoy talking to Mina.

1992: Mina and Sharon rush to Mina's parents' home after receiving an emergency call. Just as Mina's parents are in the process of moving to an apartment from their house where they had resided for 33 years, Mina's mother broke her ankle, while her father needs to undergo cancer treatment.

1992: Sharon's father is dying. Sharon and Mina go East to see him and the family. There is a lot of tension within the family. Sharon's brother acts very uptight around Mina. Sharon and Mina spend time with Sharon's father at the hospital and then return to Los Angeles. Sharon's father, age 85, dies the next day. Sharon does not return for the funeral. Later that year, Sharon and Mina return for a short visit. Her mother appears to be coping adequately, relying mostly on neighbors and people in her employ for help. Sharon's brother and sister-in-law, who live within a few blocks of their mother, talk on the phone to her daily and see her once a week. Sharon's mother is not satisfied, feeling they do not help enough.

1994: Sharon's mother, age 83, comes to Los Angeles for a visit. She decides she likes the area and feels she will receive more support and attention from Sharon and Mina. She leaves a deposit on a retirement residence. She returns home and begins to feel unwell. She cancels her rental agreement in California, and without telling Sharon she takes a series of medical tests which eventually show she has a fast-moving and fatal form of leukemia.

1995: Two months later, Sharon and Mina visit with Sharon's mother on her deathbed. She is unusually alert and seems genuinely pleased to see both Sharon and Mina. She tells Sharon that she is glad Sharon is accompanied by Mina, as she feels Mina will be of great help and support. She tells Sharon not to worry about her; she has lived a long life and knows she is dying. Her last words, spoken to Sharon, are: "Don't do like I did, living just to make money. Enjoy your life."

Sharon and Mina stay for the funeral. Sharon feels very sad, but also uplifted by her last interaction with her mother.

1995: Mina's father dies at age 80. At the funeral, the conservative rabbi includes Sharon's name as he describes various members of the immediate family. Sharon is given a black ribbon to wear at the funeral because she is considered a member of the family.

1995 and 1996: Mina spends a great deal of time traveling back and forth between Los Angeles and her mother's home to help and support her mother through the grieving process. Sharon goes with Mina on many of these visits. Mina's mother also visits in Los Angeles, especially for holidays and birthdays.

1997: Mina's mother decides to name Sharon as a beneficiary in her will should Mina's death precede her mother's. She does this because she says she believes very strongly in fairness. Both Mina and Sharon are very touched by the acceptance which is symbolized by this act.

As the authors of this account, we freely admit that our perceptions are biased, limited by our closeness to the subject matter, but we feel the following insights are worth noting and may contribute further to an understanding of lesbian life across the life cycle, as well as kinship ties.

When as a lesbian couple we first disclosed to family, there was a considerable amount of strain and tension in our relationships with family members, particularly parents and one sibling. This can be understood as the period of the revelation crisis (Strommen, 1989). As time goes on, both families settle into a comfort zone, dealing or not dealing in their own individual ways with the fact that their daughter or sister is a lesbian and in a coupled relationship with a woman. This adjustment stage (DeVine, 1984) lasted a short while for some, and for other family members it took decades before proceeding on to any kind of resolution.

The fact that both of us were known by both families as children and the fact that both of us come from the same ethnic and religious background may have added a different dimension to the family's initial perceptions. These factors probably mitigated against each family seeing the nonfamily partner in the lesbian relationship as unfamiliar and the *real* lesbian.

Mina and her parents live closer to each other than Sharon's family. Mina's parents are initially more accepting than Sharon's parents, and Mina is more willing to work hard to explain *life as a lesbian* to her parents. Mina's mother comes to fully accept Sharon as a family member. She wanted to overcome her own homophobia and was willing to listen to her daughter. Sharon makes similar attempts at explanation of lesbian life, but she does not get a "listening" response from either parents or sibling. As time goes on, Mina's parents ask questions and learn more about lesbians and the lesbian communities. Mina and Sharon become closer to Mina's parents. They are accepting and inclusive of Sharon in most of the family activities. All seem to enjoy each other's company and friendship. Sharon feels very accepted by Mina's family. DeVine's (1984) integration stage is achieved in this family.

Sharon's family is less accepting, but despite the pain of homophobia there was a willingness and a desire on the part of both parents to continue a relationship, however superficial. Sharon's parents, especially her mother, showed some acceptance of the relationship and of Mina. In spite of the conflict in Sharon's family, threats of disinheritance were not realized.

Sharon remains close to her only niece, who has recently moved West. She does not feel at all close to her brother and sister-in-law, who have never visited her in the 27 years she has lived in California.

As the parents became old, over 70 years of age, they displayed the need for emotional support from their daughters. After each father died, the surviving mother turned to her daughter for emotional and/or practical support. This response is no different than the pattern detected among mothers and daughters in the general population (Abel, 1991). Mina's mother leans heavily on Mina for support to accomplish jobs that her husband used to perform. Mina has spent much time teaching her mother to perform certain tasks; for example, balancing a checkbook, putting gas in the car, knowing when to take the car in for regular maintenance, keeping track of investments, and preparing for income tax. Two years after her father's death, Mina still speaks almost daily to her mother on the phone. Prior to his death, they spoke on average twice a week.

Sharon's involvement with her mother after her father died is more distant. They speak by phone, but the conversations were more frequent than earlier. Toward the end of her mother's life, Sharon's mother offered to buy us a larger home for the three of us to live in together. Because she never fully accepted Sharon's lesbianism or her relationship with Mina, the offer was refused. She then made arrangements to move to the same city where we live. Although this did not occur, her attempt to move closer indicates how strong her bond was with Sharon.

Sharon's decision not to have her mother move into her own home was based on Sharon's experience of her mother as nonaccepting. Social service providers and case managers involved in helping the parents of midlife lesbians should take into consideration whether the adult daughter feels accepted by the parent in question and whether or not the parent is emotionally able to accept the "out" daughter's life situation.

Acceptance or nonacceptance of midlife lesbian daughters may affect some feature of the care-giving situation. The authors speculate that assuming there are no special negative circumstances (e.g., earlier physical and/or emotional abuse), many "out" midlife lesbians do wish to play some role in helping their mothers when they are no longer able to care for themselves. The offer and acceptance of care-taking most likely is facilitated by a timely acceptance of the daughter's lesbianism.

Involvement in these care-giving activities actually may serve as a healing force in the relationship. The "integration" stage described by DeVine (1984) where the family members change their values regarding lesbianism in order to accept a new role for the daughter may not occur for some family members until late old age, perhaps in widowhood, when the lesbian daughter is the one a parent turns to for care-giving or support.

Since 1969 and the beginning of the gay liberation movement, more lesbians are "out" to family members than in earlier years; however, those who are closeted with family will encounter special problems in addressing the needs of aging parents (e.g., participation of the significant other in care-giving activities may not be possible). The closeted lesbian, unlike previous generations, may feel she is sacrificing too much of herself in order to meet her familial responsibilities. The very fact of being closeted may keep the lesbian daughter at both a physical as well as emotional distance from family.

The lesbian daughter who feels the need to be overinvolved in the lives of her aging parents might wish to explore whether or not there may be an element of trying to prove she is a "good enough" daughter or the "one" the parents can trust the most–a form of compensation for her own loss of status or role in the family.

There have been many assumptions put forth by social scientists regarding the demise of the extended family in Western society. Shanas and Sussman (1977) and Sussman and Steinmetz (1987) demonstrated that the extended family still exists in a modified and still changing form. Their findings focused on the extent of relationships and exchange of service and supports between the generations within the extended family.

Research findings often do not include any detailed information of how lesbians relate to their extended families across the generations and in the context of changing societal attitudes toward lesbianism. Although it is difficult to use large-scale empirical studies as conducted by the researchers mentioned above to investigate a population that is mostly hidden, it is possible for researchers to use smaller survey studies and in-depth case studies to investigate how extended family patterns of lesbians may change over time and between generations. The midlife lesbian's relationship pattern with family members may change from distant to one of involvement in the closing stages of the parents' lives or it may not be in the best interest of the lesbian daughter to become more involved with her parents. This is an important area of concern to social service providers who need to be apprised of the issues and implications.

REFERENCES

Abel, E. K. (1991). *Who cares for the elderly? Public policy and the experience of adult daughters.* Philadelphia: Temple University Press.

Adelman, M. (1991). Stigma, gay lifestyles, and adjustment to aging: A study of later-life gay men and lesbians. In J. A. Lee (Ed.), *Gay midlife and maturity* (pp. 7-32). New York: The Haworth Press, Inc.

Berger, R. (1982). *Gay and gray: The older homosexual man.* Urbana: University of Illinois Press.

Brown, L. S. (1988). Lesbians, gay men and their families: Common clinical issues. *Journal of Gay and Lesbian Psychotherapy, 1,* 65-77.

Cass, V. (1979). Homosexual identity formation: A theoretical model. *Journal of Homosexuality, 4,* 219-236.

Cass, V. (1984). Homosexual identity: A concept in need of definition. *Journal of Homosexuality, 9,* (2/3), 105-126.

DeMonteflores, C., & Schultz, S. (1978). Coming out: Similarities and differences for lesbians and gay men. *The Journal of Social Issues, 34,* 59-72.

DeVine, J. L. (1984). A systematic inspection of affectional preference orientation and the family of origin. *Journal of Social Work and Human Sexuality, 2,* 9-17.

Greene, B. (1994). Lesbian and gay sexual orientations: Implications for clinical training, practice, and research. In B. Greene & G. Herek (Eds.), *Lesbian and gay psychology: Theory, research, and clinical applications* (pp. 1-24). Thousand Oaks, CA: Sage.

Hoffman, D. (Producer & Director). (1994). *Complaints of a dutiful daughter* [Film]. (Available from Women Make Movies, A D/D Production, New York, NY)

Japenga, A. (1987, February 13). Love stories. *Los Angeles Times,* View Section 1.

Johnson, S. (1990). *Staying power: Long term lesbian couples.* Tallahassee: Naiad Press.

Minnigerode, F., & Adelman, M. (1978). Elderly homosexual women and men: Report on a pilot study. *The Family Coordinator,* October, 451-456.

Norris, J. (1998). *Daughters of the elderly.* Bloomington: Indiana University Press.

Plummer, K. (1975). *Sexual stigma: An interactionist account.* London/Boston: Routledge and Kegan Paul, Ltd.

Raphael, S., & Robinson, M. (1984). The older lesbian: Love relationships and friendship patterns. In T. Darty & S. Potter (Eds.), *Women-identified women* (pp. 67-82). Palo Alto, CA: Mayfield.

Robinson, M. a.k.a. Meyer, M. (1979). The older lesbian. Unpublished master's thesis, California State University Dominguez Hills, Cason, CA.

Shanas, E., Townsend, P., & Stehouwer, J. (Eds.). (1968). *Old people in three industrial societies.* New York: Atherton Press.

Shanas, E., & Sussman, M. (Eds.). (1977). *Family, bureaucracy and the elderly.* Durham: University Press.

Somers, T., & Shields, L. (1987). *Women take care.* Gainesville: Triad Publishing.

Strommen, E. L. (1989). Hidden branches and growing pains: Stressful aspects of negotiating their lives: Homosexuality and the family tree. *Marriage & Family Review, 14,* 9-34.

Sussman, M., & Steinmetz, S. (Eds.). (1987). *Handbook of marriage and family.* New York: Plenum Press.

Warshow, J. (1991). How lesbian identity affects the mother/daughter relationship. In B. Sang, J. Warshow, & A. Smith (Eds.), *Lesbians at midlife: The creative transition* (pp. 80-83). San Francisco: Spinsters Book Company.

Weinberg, T. S. (1983). *Gay men, gay selves: The social construction of homosexual identities.* New York: Irvington.

Index

AA. *See* Alcoholics Anonymous
Abandonment issues, with parental
    death, 54,56,62
Acceptance factors
    age as, 5,25,53,141-143
    caretaking impact of, 140-143,149
    parenting and, 5,53,58,129-130,
        135-136
    of romantic relationships, 5-6,12
Adolescence
    dating and courtship in, 77-102
    partnerships in, 82-84
Adoption, as parenting option, 121,
    129,131
Adult development. *See*
    Developmental process
Adulthood. *See also* Midlife; Young
    adulthood
    dating and courtship in, 77-102
    societal markers of, 6
Age and aging
    as acceptance factor, 5,25,53,140
    bereavement and, 50,54,71
    caretaking and, 20,140-143
    coming out and, 25,51-53,82
    courtship impact of, 82-84,98-100
    midlife impact of, 121-122, 140-143
    as stigma, 6-7,45,121
    subjectivity and, 50-51
AIDS, friends lost to, 113
Alcohol abuse. *See* Chemical
    dependency
Alcoholics Anonymous (AA)
    as support network, 109-110
    women in, 111-115
Alliances, primary *versus* multiple, 24
Alternative-family camps, 39
Alternative insemination, 45,120
Alternative parenting. *See* Lesbian
    mothers; Parenting

Ambivalence, parental death and, 54,
    58
Assertion. *See* Coming out
Authenticity, midlife dynamics of,
    51-52,68

Baby boom, 45, 120, 135
Bereavement
    filial. *See* Parental death
    personal growth through, 40,50-55
Best friends, expectations of, 17-24,83
Birthing, as parenting option, 121,126,
    129,131
Bisexuals. *See* LGBTs
Body language, for courtship
    initiation, 81
Bonding, as parenting issue, 124,
    126-127,133-134
Boundaries, personal, 108,123

Careers
    couples' challenges with, 37,41,116
    as identity component, 13,20,24,
        36,83
    midlife changes in, 37,68,112,116
    parenting and, 120,126,128,131,
        135
Caregivers
    acceptance factors for, 140-143,149
    family as, 20,122,140-143
    formal service systems of. *See*
        Counseling; Health care
        providers
    friends as, 10-11
    midlife couples as, 38-40,140-143
        case example of, 139,143-150
Caretaking. *See* Caregivers
Case examples